War and Warfare

Inside ANCIENT GREECE

War and Warfare

ANNE WRIGHT

Sharpe Focus

an imprint of M.E. Sharpe, Inc.

First edition for the United States, its territories and dependencies,
Canada, Mexico, and Australia, published in 2008 by M.E. Sharpe, Inc.

Sharpe Focus
An imprint of M.E. Sharpe, Inc.
80 Business Park Drive
Armonk, NY 10504

www.mesharpe.com

Library of Congress Cataloging-in-Publication Data

Wright, Anne Margaret.
    War and warfare / Anne Wright.
        p. cm. -- (Inside ancient Greece)
    Includes bibliographical references and index.
    ISBN 978-0-7656-8133-1 (hardcover : alk. paper)
    1. Military art and science--Greece--History--To 1500--Juvenile
literature. 2. Naval art and science--Greece--Juvenile literature. 3.
Greece--History, Military--To 146 B.C.--Juvenile literature. I. Title.

U33.W75 2008
938--dc22
                                2007011422

Editorial and design by Amber Books Ltd
Project Editor: James Bennett
Copy Editor: Deborah Murrell
Picture Research: Kate Green
Design: Andrew Easton

Cover Design: Jesse Sanchez, M.E. Sharpe, Inc.

Printed in Malaysia

9 8 7 6 5 4 3 2 1

For four great St. Andrews friends: Alex, Elspeth, Susanna and Victoria.

PICTURE CREDITS
AKG-Images: 6–7, 8, 13, 14, 16, 17, 18, 20, 27, 31, 32, 36, 39, 42, 45, 51, 56, 58, 59, 62, 63, 72–73
Bridgeman Art Library: 34, 60
Corbis: 22, 37
De Agostini: 10, 12, 24, 26, 33, 40, 44, 49, 50, 55, 70, 74(both), 75
Getty Images: 21, 66
J B Illustrations/Amber Books: 28–29, 52–53, 64–65
Mary Evans Picture Library: 46, 69

ABOUT THE AUTHOR
Anne Wright gained a First Class Honours degree from the University of St. Andrews, Scotland,
before moving on to further study at Corpus Christi College, University of Oxford. After teaching in
London, she moved back to Oxford, where she is currently Head of Classics at Summer Fields, an
independent boys' boarding school. She lives in Oxford, U.K.

Contents

Introduction

The civilization of the ancient Greeks has influenced the world for thousands of years. Much of what we take for granted today, in areas such as science, mathematics, drama, poetry, and philosophy, was invented by the ancient Greeks. In many other fields, too, the Greeks made huge advances in human knowledge. Modern politicians still look for inspiration to fifth-century B.C.E. Athens, the cradle of democracy. Ancient Greek plays are still performed today, and in all the major cities of the world you can find buildings heavily influenced by Greek architecture. This series of books explores the full richness of Greek culture and history. It also considers how Greek civilization still influences us today.

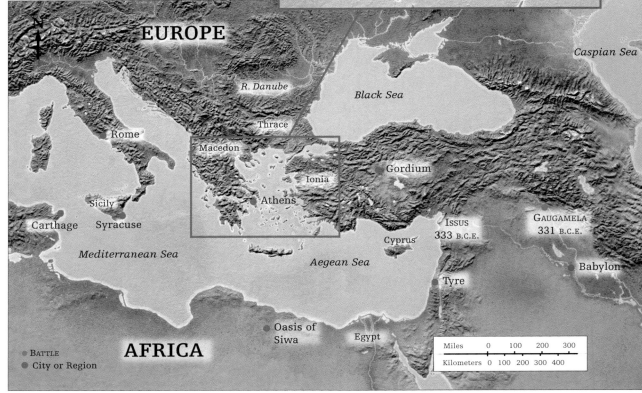

War in Ancient Greece

In ancient times, Greece was not united into one country as it is today, but was divided up into many different city-states. Greek city-states were fiercely competitive and very independent-minded. This desire for independence often led to conflict, and meant that wars were common events. *War and Warfare* tells the story of some of the great wars that the Greeks fought. The Persian Wars in the early fifth century B.C.E. were fought against the much larger Persian Empire. The Peloponnesian War, in the late fifth century B.C.E., was fought between the two city-states of Athens and Sparta, and their allies. In the fourth century B.C.E., Alexander the Great led a large army into Asia and conquered a vast amount of land, stretching from Egypt to Afghanistan. Finally, the rise of Rome marked the end of Greek independence.

Many of these ancient clashes, such as the Battle of Thermopylae, when King Leonidas and 300 brave Greek troops fought to the death against an invading Persian army, are still famous today.

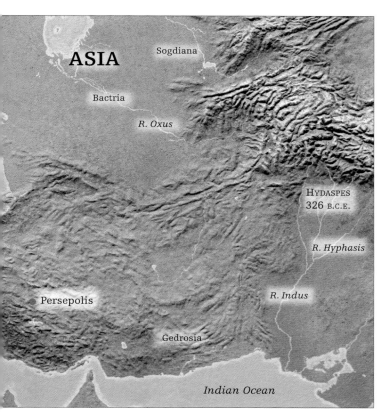

As well as narrating the history of the great wars, this book also discusses the equipment and organization of the Greek armies. The main fighting forces were cavalry and infantry, but the Greeks also used war elephants, siege-engines, and catapults. Naval combat was also a very important part of Greek warfare, partly because much of Greece is surrounded by sea. All of these elements played their part in the various wars and battles of the ancient Greeks.

This map shows some of the key states in ancient Greece and the sites of some of the most important battles.

Chapter One

Early Warfare

When we think of Greece, we tend to think of the modern state, which is a united country with the capital in Athens. However, ancient Greece was very different. Instead of one country called Greece, there were a great number of individual city-states, such as Athens, Sparta, and Corinth. These city-states were made up of a town center and the agricultural land surrounding it. Some city-states were more powerful than others and these tended to have political influence over their weaker neighbors. However, all the city-states were eager to preserve their independence and their right to make their own decisions; and because there were hundreds of city-states in ancient Greece, it was very difficult for neighboring states always to agree. This meant that local rivalry often spilled over into armed conflict. In fact, a year without a quarrel between city-states in some part of the Greek world was most unusual. Thus, the Greeks regarded war as a normal part of life. They recognized the difficulties and dangers of war, but they also believed that war could not always be avoided.

Equipment

Greek soldiers used a wide range of equipment. Different types of soldiers wore different armor and carried different weapons. The aim was to be as lethally armed as possible, while also being well-protected. Military equipment changed over time as

Greek soldiers fought in line, a formation known as the phalanx. This modern illustration shows a line of Spartan warriors fighting at the Battle of Thermopylae in 480 B.C.E.

The bronze Corinthian helmet was the most common type of head protector from the eighth to the fifth centuries B.C.E. It had a linen or leather lining.

experience in war drove forward military technology. However, there were certain basic types of equipment, which most Greek soldiers used in one form or another. These were helmets, shields, body armor, spears, and daggers.

Helmets

The earliest helmets from Mycenaean times were made from boars' tusks and leather. Male boars grow long, sharp tusks. Early Greeks cut these tusks into small, thin plates and sewed them in rows onto a leather cap. To provide enough plates to cover an entire helmet required the tusks from ten or more boars. Bronze cheek pieces were also attached to the helmet to ensure that most of the face was protected.

By the eighth century B.C.E., helmets were made of bronze. The most common type was the Corinthian helmet. This kind of helmet covered the wearer's entire face, apart from eye-slits and an opening for the mouth. Later helmets sometimes also had the area around the ear cut out to allow the wearer to hear properly. Bronze helmets were heavy, and were lined with leather or linen to make them more comfortable and less likely to slip on the head. Helmets were essential for protecting a soldier's head, but they also had another role: to induce fear in the opponent.

With his face enclosed in a mask of bronze, a soldier did not look like a normal human being. This effect was enhanced by the use of crests. These were plumes of horsehair attached to the top of the helmet. The crests were often dyed bright colors, and they made the wearer appear taller and more terrifying than he actually was.

Shields

In early warfare there appears to have been two types of shields, each of which was made from leather stretched over a wooden frame. Figure-of-eight shields were shaped like the figure eight, with rounded rims. "Tower" shields were much larger and heavier to carry.

Why Were Shields Decorated?

Hoplite shields were usually decorated. Sometimes symbols were used to show which city-state a hoplite came from. For example, Spartans carried shields with a capital "L" on them. This stood for Lacedaemon (*Lass-ee-DIE-mon*), the Spartan name for Sparta. At other times, shield decoration was drawn from mythology and was designed to terrify the enemy. To see a gorgon (a hideous monster with snakes for hair) approaching at a swift pace must have been terrifying, even if you knew that there was only a man carrying it!

In the eighth or seventh century B.C.E., a new shield type appears to have been introduced. This was the prototype of the hoplite shield, which was carried by heavily armed infantry solders, or hoplites. This circular shield was made of oak planks with a bronze sheet covering the outer face. The shield had a leather lining, a leather arm-loop, and a hand grip. The shield was very heavy, so soldiers often rested the rim of the shield on their shoulder.

Body Armor

The earliest example of body armor to survive dates from the fifteenth century B.C.E., and consists of hoops of bronze joined together. There were also two shoulder guards and a collar-like neck piece. Military technology clearly developed over the next seven centuries, but there is no archaeological evidence for exactly what happened. The next oldest example of body armor dates to the late eighth century. By this point, the breastplate was made up of a back and a front piece, tied together. The breastplate was shaped like a man's torso and provided protection for the upper body. It also had a leather lining to make it much more comfortable to wear. Bronze armor was expensive to produce and only the rich could afford new armor, which was made to fit them. Poorer soldiers probably made do with secondhand equipment.

In the late sixth century, the bronze breastplate became less common. Instead, body armor consisted of layers of stiffened linen called a *cuirass* (*kew-rass*), to which metal scales might be added. Linen strips also hung down from the tunic. The advantages of the cuirass were that it was much cheaper and lighter than a bronze breastplate, and it enabled the wearer to move more quickly.

Most breastplates were made out of stiffened linen. This iron breastplate belonged to King Philip II of Macedon and was decorated with gold.

A soldier usually wore leg protectors called *greaves*. These were made from a thin sheet of bronze, shaped to fit around the shins. Sometimes soldiers also wore arm protectors, but these seem to have been much less common than leg greaves. Hoplites would not have worn boots, but would have had leather sandals.

Spears

In the poems of Homer, heroes threw spears at each other as if they were javelins. However, evidence from later ancient Greek authors is that spears were used for thrusting, not throwing. Spears had a wooden shaft around 6 to 8 feet (1.8–2.4 meters) long, with an iron spearhead. There was a spike on the bottom of the shaft called a butt-spike. This was essential to properly balance the weapon. The butt-spike could also be driven into the ground. This meant that a soldier did not have to hold a heavy weapon while waiting for a battle to start. Finally, the butt-spike could be used as a second weapon if the top half of the spear broke off. When soldiers fought in formation, it was essential to take care not to spear other members of the formation with the butt-spike, which pointed backward into the ranks and could easily blind or kill a friend.

Other Weapons

Soldiers also carried daggers and swords. These were not used in the first wave of a battle, but were very useful in hand-to-hand fighting when squadrons of infantry had lost their formation. Bows and arrows were used in Mycenaean times—the period between 1600 and 1100 B.C.E.—and

Helmets had crests to make the wearer seem taller and more ferocious.

The Corinthian helmet was made of bronze and protected the head and face.

Spears were made of iron fixed onto a wooden shaft.

Spartan hoplites were easily identifiable by their red cloaks.

Shields were made of wood with a bronze facing. They were heavy, but soldiers could rest the inner rim of the shield on their shoulder. It was the mark of a coward to lose his shield on the battlefield. Spartan mothers told their sons to come back with their shields or to be brought back dead on top of them.

This representation shows how a Spartan hoplite (or heavily armed soldier) would have been armed around 500 B.C.E. His main weapon was his spear, but he would use his sword if the spear broke.

The bottom of the spear had a sharp spike known as a butt-spike. This enabled the spear to be stuck in the ground while the soldier waited in line. It also made a good weapon if the spear shaft broke.

Bronze greaves protected the shins and knees from attack.

Soldiers wore simple sandals on their feet.

13

were also employed by one of the Greeks' main enemies, the Persians. Archers could fire large numbers of arrows at attacking troops. Although the Persians regularly used archers, the standard Greek body armor provided good protection against arrows. Moreover, archers did not wear armor, so they were easily slaughtered by heavily armed soldiers.

Homeric Warfare

Although there is archaeological evidence for armor dating back to the fifteenth century B.C.E., there is no written evidence about warfare until the poems of Homer in the eighth century B.C.E. The *Iliad* (*ILL-ee-ad*) tells the tale of the war between the Greeks and the Trojans. However, while the *Iliad* is an exciting war story, it seems unlikely that Greek warfare was fought quite in the manner it describes. In particular, the *Iliad* focuses on what important noblemen do, and ignores the pitched battles of lesser-ranking troops. It is likely that the *Iliad* presents an idealized picture of Homeric warfare, and it should not be assumed that war was really like this either in the time of the Trojan War or in the eighth century.

Mycenaean warriors were armed with either large "tower" shields or figure-of-eight shields. This representation shows a warrior getting ready to drive into battle. He is wearing a very early form of body armor.

The Dark Ages

Around the twelfth century B.C.E., Greece entered a Dark Age. Archaeological artifacts show that Greece became much poorer, but there is no written material from the Dark Ages, so it is difficult to reconstruct exactly what happened during this time. Battles seem to have been fought with cavalry and infantry, but there does not appear to have been an organized phalanx. It seems likely that most wars occurred over squabbles about who controlled land.

Certainly, later Greek writers believed that the first real, historical war (as opposed to the legendary warfare of Homer's poetry) was a contest about who should control the rich

Homeric Heroes

The Homeric hero drove up to the battlefield in a chariot, wearing a boar's tusk helmet and full armor, and carrying a shield. Heroes fought in single combat with spears and then closed in to finish off their opponent with swords. Some aspects of Homeric warfare were very different from later warfare. Cavalry charges did not take place and, although Troy was under siege, there were no attempts to capture the city by destroying its walls. In Homer, the chariot was a means of transport, but in fourth century B.C.E. Persia, chariots were weapons of war with scythes on their wheels to cut people down.

agricultural land of the Lelantine (*Leh-lan-tine*) Plain. This war was called the Lelantine War and it occurred in the eighth century B.C.E. between Chalcis (*Kal-kiss*) and Eretria (*Eh-ret-REE-ah*), two states on the island of Euboea (*YOU-bee-uh*). Very little is known about it other than that both states claimed the right to the Lelantine Plain. It is not even known who won.

Organization

In early Greek history, infantry troops appear to have fought as a disorganized mass, without any special training. However, in the eighth or seventh century B.C.E., a deadly new military

The War-cry or Paean

Greek troops tended to sing a paean (*pai-an*) before a battle started. The paean was a kind of war-cry or war-song, where the troops called on the gods to help them. At the Battle of Salamis, in 480 B.C.E., the Persians thought that the Greeks were retreating. However, the Greeks began to sing the paean in a triumphant, not a frightened, manner. At that point the Persians realized that the Greeks expected victory and it was the Persians who became afraid.

machine came into being: the hoplite phalanx (*fah-lancs*). Hoplites were heavily armored infantrymen and the phalanx was a new method of organizing them into a square or rectangular formation. The hoplites marched together in lines, thus ensuring that each soldier was protected by his and his neighbor's shield. The weight of the heavy infantry was used to break through opposing formations and the phalanx was lethal when directed against troops who were not drawn up in a phalanx formation. Moreover, cavalry were of little use against a phalanx that kept its formation. Horses cannot charge through a

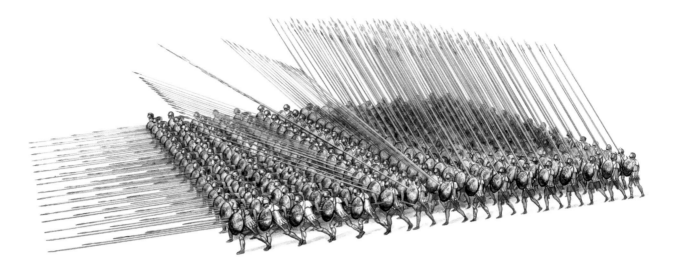

A phalanx was very difficult to attack head-on and was lethal when matched against non-phalanx formations of infantry.

solid mass of spears, and this was to be of great benefit to the Greeks when they fought armies strong in cavalry. The phalanx was modified by King Philip II of Macedon, who introduced the *sarissa* (*suh-RISS-uh*), or Macedonian spear. This was longer than the traditional hoplite spear and meant that the phalanx was even more lethal than before, because there were more spear points in the front line. Philip also introduced the use of lightly armed troops called *peltasts*, who were used as skirmishers.

The Campaigning Season

In all the wars in Greece, the harsh terrain caused difficulties. There were no modern roads and it was extremely hard to move through the passes and mountains in winter. The seas were also rough and stormy after autumn. Therefore, campaigning and battles tended to take place in the spring and summer months. Moreover, with the exception of the Spartans, the Greek soldiers were not professionals. It was essential that they had time to get in the harvest if they were to have enough food to live on during the coming year.

Cavalry

Cavalry were not as important as infantry in Greek warfare. This was partly because cavalry were very expensive to equip and partly because most of Greece is not flat enough for effective cavalry use. Cavalry were normally deployed in a square formation, but Alexander the Great changed this into a wedge-shaped arrangement. The tip of the wedge was able to crash through the enemy line and drive a hole into it, which the infantry phalanx could then attack. The Macedonian cavalry formation was also very maneuverable and could easily change direction, wheeling around to attack the enemy from virtually any angle.

Sieges

Although many Greek wars were decided on the battlefield, sometimes an entire population might retreat behind their city's walls and try to sit out a siege. Siege warfare was extremely expensive for the attacking side (for example, Athens spent more on the siege of Samos in 440 B.C.E. than on building the Parthenon).

The essential equipment for withstanding a siege was a strong set of city walls. The population would retreat behind the walls for safety, also bringing in their animals and treasure. The walls at Mycenae were built in the second half of the fourteenth century B.C.E. and are an example of some of the earliest fortifications in Greece. In fact, the walls were built of such large blocks of stone that they were called cyclopean, because it was thought that only a race of giants (or cyclopes) could have constructed them. Mycenae also had a water reservoir to enable the city to withstand long sieges.

Although ingenious siege machines were designed to help to capture besieged cities, most city-states in fact fell through treachery from inside, rather than being captured by the attackers.

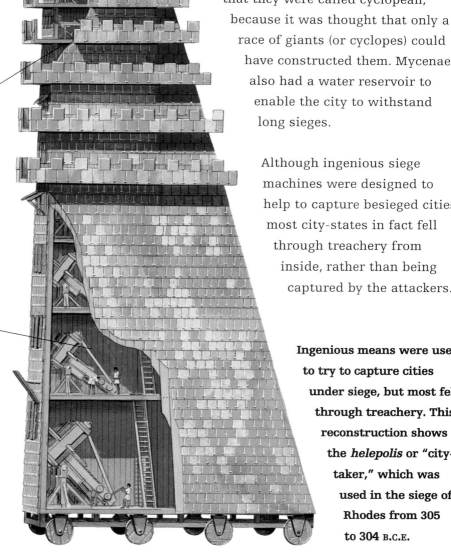

The "city-taker" was 141 feet (43 meters) high and 200 men were needed to push it forward.

Men placed in the top two floors used bolt-throwing catapults to shoot troops defending the besieged city.

Men on the bottom two floors operated large stone-throwing catapults. The stones may have weighed up to 180 pounds (80 kilograms) and were used to break down the city walls.

Ingenious means were used to try to capture cities under siege, but most fell through treachery. This reconstruction shows the *helepolis* or "city-taker," which was used in the siege of Rhodes from 305 to 304 B.C.E.

Triremes might deliberately ram into another ship to break off one set of oars. Once a trireme had been disabled it was unable to maneuver and would easily fall victim to an attacking ship.

Naval Warfare

Greek ships had developed over the centuries. The original warship was the *pentecontor* (*pen-teh-con-tor*), which had fifty oars. By the fifth century B.C.E., the basic unit was the highly maneuverable *trireme* (*tri-reem*), which had 170 rowers, arranged in three banks of oars. Triremes also had sails, but these were brought down during battles.

Triremes could be used for carrying out raids on enemy territory, but were also very important in pitched sea battles. The trireme

The Corinthian Navy

The city-state of Corinth was situated in a strategic position at the crossroads of the east-west sea route through the Gulf of Corinth and the north-south land route from central Greece into the Peloponnese. Corinth had been active in overseas trade and colonization since the eighth century B.C.E. By the seventh century B.C.E., Corinth was both rich and powerful. Part of her wealth was channeled into the development of her navy. By the end of the sixth century B.C.E., Corinth had a fleet of about seventy ships, one of the largest fleets at that time. Corinth continued to be one of the most powerful states at sea until the fifth century B.C.E., when Athens overtook her.

Methods of Waging War

Chariots

War chariots were pulled by four horses and could move quickly across a battlefield. They had scythes—long, curved blades—fitted onto their wheels. However, although the Persians used war chariots, they were uncommon in Greece, where the land was unsuitable.

Elephants

War elephants were regularly used by Indian kings, and Greek rulers started to use them regularly in the late fourth century B.C.E. Horses were terrified by the smell of elephants and had to be specially trained to approach them. However, elephants were not easy to control and could wreak havoc on their own side if they charged out of position and crashed through the troops drawn up behind them.

Catapults

From the fourth century B.C.E., Greek armies used torsion catapults, which had a spring of sinew, rope, or hair. The rope was twisted around and around before the catapult was loaded. When the spring was released, the power was such that it could send an iron bolt through a column of men nearly a quarter of a mile (0.5 kilometers) away. Catapults were most commonly used in sieges to hurl rocks against city walls.

had a reinforced prow, which enabled it to ram an enemy ship at high speed, reverse out from the stricken vessel, and leave it to sink. Another common tactic was to sail up to an enemy ship and use the ram to smash through the oars on one side of it. This maneuver required split-second timing because it was vital to pull in the oars before they struck the enemy ship.

The Rise of Sparta

One of the most important changes in early Greece was the rise of Sparta. Until the seventh century B.C.E., Sparta had not been especially powerful. However, in the late eighth century, she defeated the nearby state of Messenia (*Mess-EE-nee-uh*) and enslaved the inhabitants. These enslaved people were called Helots, and were forced to work for the Spartans on the land. Sparta grew richer, but at first did not become more powerful in military terms. Soon Sparta was in conflict with the state of Argos, and was defeated in 669 B.C.E. Around 630 B.C.E., the Helots revolted against Spartan rule and it took the Spartans seventeen years to regain full control.

The Spartans realized that they had to both defend themselves from invasion and make sure that the Helots could not rebel again. They did this by creating a unique system of military

The Spartans Comb Their Hair

The Spartans had a fearsome reputation for courage throughout Greece. Spartan soldiers were trained to the strictest discipline from childhood and were unmatched in terms of skill and experience. However, for some time the Persian king, Xerxes (*ZERK-seez*), thought that their reputation was exaggerated. In 480 B.C.E., before the Battle of Thermopylae (*Thur-MOP-ee-lie*), a scout reported to Xerxes that the Spartan soldiers were combing their hair. Xerxes thought that this was a very womanly action and that proper soldiers would not behave in such a fashion. However, Spartans only combed their hair before a dangerous battle, and events soon forced Xerxes to change his mind about their courage.

Spartan soldiers were the most feared of all Greek soldiers. They were highly disciplined and were very difficult to defeat. This is a Greek sculpture of a Spartan soldier from the fifth century B.C.E.

training for every Spartan citizen. This would not have been possible without the Helots. Since the Helots cultivated the land and produced the food, Spartan citizens did not have to spend time looking after their farms or harvesting their crops. Instead, they were free to spend their time training to be soldiers. Thus, the Spartans created the first professional army in Greece.

Over time, Sparta extended her influence in the Peloponnese, uniting various states in the region into the Peloponnesian League, under Spartan leadership. By the late sixth century B.C.E., Sparta was the strongest state on mainland Greece. However, development in

The Three Ranks of Spartan Society

The people who lived in Sparta were divided up into three groups. First came the full Spartan citizens, or Spartiates. The Perioikoi (*Per-EE-oi-koi*) were the second group. While the Perioikoi (or "dwellers round about") were not full Spartan citizens, they had some independence and were allowed to take part in trade. They did, however, have to provide soldiers to fight alongside the Spartans in battle. The final group were the Helots, who acted as slaves to the Spartiates.

Greece was not just restricted to Sparta. Corinth had a very strong fleet of ships and had built up a network of colonies in northwest Greece. Athens became much stronger in the mid-sixth

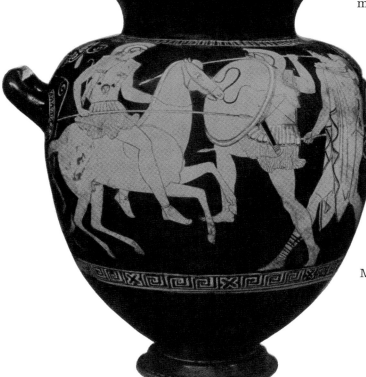

century under her ruler, Pisistratus (*Pie-SIS-trah-tuss*). Pisistratus stopped much of the political rivalry in Athens, encouraged peace, and established a system of law courts. This helped to stimulate trade which, in turn, brought increasing wealth to Athens. By the beginning of the fifth century, Sparta, Corinth, and Athens were all important states, with links throughout the Greek world. Their strength, however, was soon to be tested by the most powerful empire in the Mediterranean region—Persia.

This fifth-century Greek vase shows a cavalryman attacking infantry.

Chapter Two

The Persian Wars

In the early fifth century B.C.E., the greatest power in the Mediterranean region was Persia. Persian influence had originally been confined to part of modern Iran, but it soon expanded to include the whole Middle East. At the height of its power, the Persian Empire stretched from Egypt to India and Afghanistan. Persia controlled a region that was about seventy times larger than the territory of the Greek city-states. Therefore, when Persia came into conflict with these quarrelsome Greek city-states on her borders, no one would have expected her to be defeated. Yet she was.

The Rise of Persia

Under the rule of the Persian king Cyrus the Great, Persian power expanded greatly. Not only did Cyrus add much of Assyria and Babylonia to Persian territory, but in 546 B.C.E. he also conquered the kingdom of Lydia, in the western half of modern Turkey. This conquest was very important to the Greeks, because there were many Greek cities on the coastal fringes of Ionia, ruled by Lydia. Although these Ionian city-states were swapping one ruler for another, they were unhappy with the change. The king of Lydia, Croesus (*KREE-suss*), had been a generous ruler. He respected the Greek way of life and had honored the Greek gods, giving lavish gifts to their temples. The Greeks realized that Cyrus would not be so supportive. Moreover, they had refused to help Cyrus against Croesus, and they knew that he was angry with them and did not trust them.

This painting shows a Greek hoplite carrying a heavy shield and armed with a spear. In art, Greek soldiers are often shown wearing few clothes, but in reality they would have worn a tunic and a breastplate, as well as greaves to protect the legs.

Medes and Persians: The Rulers of the Near and Middle East

In the early sixth century B.C.E., the Near and Middle East were split into four regions ruled by different states. Most of what is now modern Egypt was controlled by the state of Egypt. However, some of it was ruled by Babylonia, which also ruled part of Assyria (modern Syria and Palestine). The capital of Babylonia was Babylon. The western half of modern Turkey was controlled by the kingdom of Lydia, whose capital was at Sardis. The eastern half of modern Turkey, the remainder of Assyria, and modern Iran were controlled by the Medes.

The Medes and Persians were very similar people, but to start with the Medes were more powerful and the Persians were merely a less important tribe within the kingdom of Media. However, in 550 B.C.E. a Persian, Cyrus the Great, had defeated the Medes and seized control of Media. From then on the region was known as Persia and the empire that Cyrus and his successors created was called the Persian Empire.

This limestone carving shows King Darius seated on his throne. The palace at Persepolis, the capital of the Persian Empire, was decorated with many such carvings to remind subjects of the importance of the king.

Cyrus the Great died in 529 B.C.E. and was succeeded by his son Cambyses (*Cam-BYE-seez*), who invaded and conquered Egypt in 525 B.C.E. Cambyses died in 522 B.C.E. and, after some internal squabbles, his cousin Darius became king. Darius spent the first years of his reign putting down revolts, but by 519 B.C.E. he had a secure hold over Persia and had also gained control of the Punjab in India. In 513 B.C.E., Darius became interested in expanding further westward. He led an army across the Hellespont into Europe and marched north to the mouth of the Danube River. Although he returned to Persia, he gained control of Thrace (part of modern Bulgaria) and soon controlled most of the islands in the Aegean Sea.

The Ionian Revolt, 499–494 B.C.E.

The Persians did not rule the Ionian city-states directly. Instead, they chose Greek rulers, who acted on their behalf and were responsible for maintaining the laws and ensuring that taxes were paid to the Persian Empire. However, many of the Ionian Greeks disliked this situation. They did not want to pay taxes to the Persian Empire, they resented being ruled more harshly than before, and they wanted to be independent, not part of an empire. It was not long before the Greeks were plotting to rebel against the Persians.

The Ionian Greeks knew that the Persians were far more powerful than they were and that they had vast numbers of troops at their disposal. Therefore, the Greeks decided that they must gain help. The obvious place to ask for help was mainland Greece. Ambassadors were sent to try to make alliances with certain mainland Greek states, and to gain pledges of support. At first, they were not successful. The Spartan king, Cleomenes (*KLEE-oh-men-eez*), had some sympathy for the Ionians, but refused to help when he learned that it took three months to travel from the Ionian city-states to the Persian capital, Persepolis (*Per-SEP-oh-liss*). Only the Athenians and the small state of Eretria offered to help. Athens sent twenty ships and Eretria sent five.

Once the whole fleet was assembled, the Ionians began the revolt. They attacked the regional capital, Sardis, and burned much of the city, although they did not manage to capture the citadel. The Persians were determined to crush the revolt and soon attacked the Greeks near Ephesus. The Greeks were defeated and the Athenians returned to Athens, although the Eretrians remained. The Persians were now on the offensive and moved against each individual city-state, defeating them one at a time. By 494 B.C.E., many of the Ionian city-states had been overwhelmed and Greek morale was very low. They decided to fight a sea battle near the island of Lade (*LA-day*). The Ionians lacked good leadership and the ships of several city-states deserted. The Greeks were crushed. The Persians burned the temple of Apollo at Didyma (*DID-ee-muh*) and enslaved the inhabitants of Miletus (*My-LEE-tuss*), which had once been the strongest Ionian city. The Ionian revolt was over.

The ruins of the temple of Apollo at Didyma, which was burned by the Persians in revenge for the Ionian Greeks' attack on Sardis.

Revenge

Although the Persians had crushed the Ionian revolt, they were not yet finished with the Greeks. Darius had been very angry that any of the mainland Greeks had dared to send help to the Ionian rebels and he believed that the Athenians were responsible for the burning of Sardis. The historian Herodotus (*Her-OH-duh-tuss*) records that Darius was so determined to have his revenge that he ordered a slave to say to him every night at dinner, "Master, remember the Athenians." Soon Darius was drawing up plans for an expedition into Greece to punish the Greeks for supporting the Ionians.

The First Invasion of Greece, 492 B.C.E.

Darius ordered his son-in-law, Mardonius (*Mar-DOE-nee-uss*), to lead the Persian army into Greece. There were two ways to invade Greece from Persia. Either Mardonius could cross the Hellespont, work his way around the north of Greece, and then make his way south, or he could sail across the Aegean Sea with all of his forces. To start with, Mardonius invaded Greece from the north. He soon conquered Thrace and Macedonia. However, his ships were trapped in a gale and wrecked as he attempted to navigate around the treacherous Athos promontory. Foiled by the winds, Mardonius retreated and prepared for a second attempt in 490 B.C.E.

King Darius sent ambassadors to visit the free Greek states and demand that they submit to his authority. Many of the city-states submitted, particularly those island states which Darius could easily attack. However, Sparta, the most powerful Greek city-state, refused to acknowledge Darius' authority, and killed the ambassadors. In some ways, Darius' demand had backfired. Previously, he could claim that he was punishing Athens and Eretria because they had interfered in a region that he controlled. However, by demanding that the whole of Greece acknowledge his position as overlord, he was forcing the Greeks to choose whether or not they wanted to be part of the Persian Empire. The war had widened from the Ionian Greeks to include the whole of Greece.

The Battle of Marathon, 490 B.C.E.

In 490 B.C.E., the Persians sailed across the Aegean Sea and reached the island of Euboea, where they besieged the city-state of Eretria. Eretria begged Athens to help. The Athenians agreed to do so, but believed that just two states were not enough to defeat the Persian force of 25,000 infantry and 1,000 cavalry. They asked Sparta for help, but the Spartans were celebrating a religious festival during which they were not allowed to fight. They promised to send help as soon as the festival was over, but, until then, Athens and Eretria were on their own.

The Persian forces were split into two groups. The smaller group besieged Eretria. The larger group landed on the mainland in the bay of

This fifth-century B.C.E. vase shows a battle between Greek soldiers and Persian cavalry.

Marathon, 26 miles (42 kilometers) northeast of Athens. Eight thousand Athenian infantrymen marched to Marathon where they were joined by 1,000 soldiers from Plataea (*Plat-EE-uh*). Plataea was a local city-state with friendly links to Athens. These 1,000 hoplites represented her entire citizen army. Eretria soon fell through treachery to the Persians. They destroyed it and enslaved the inhabitants. The entire Persian force was now free to attack the Athenians.

The Athenians had ten generals and a chief general, Callimachus (*Kal-IM-uh-kuss*). They had to decide whether to attack the Persians before the remaining Persian troops arrived from Eretria, or to delay in the hope that Spartan reinforcements would arrive before the Persians attacked them. Five generals were in favor of an immediate attack, but five wished to delay. Callimachus gave the casting vote in favor of attack and put the general Miltiades (*Mill-TIE-uh-deez*) in charge.

Spreading the News of Invasion

Ancient Greece lacked the modern roads used today. Often tracks wound through the mountains and were too steep for horses to climb. Therefore, the quickest means of communication was a specially trained runner. When the Athenians begged Sparta to help them at the Battle of Marathon, they sent a runner called Pheidippides (*Fie-DIP-ee-deez*). It took him two days to cover 150 miles (240 kilometers) of mountainous terrain in exhausting heat. On his way back he thought that he saw the god Pan, who promised that the Athenians would have help.

Miltiades was heavily outnumbered, so he had to create a plan that did not rely on strength of numbers. First, he used the lay of the land to help him. There were two marshes on the Plain of Marathon. The Great Marsh was too close to the Persian forces to be used as a base, but he could use the Little Marsh and the sea to protect his rear and right flank. Positioning himself near the Little Marsh also meant that he had hills to his rear, which would make it difficult for the Persians to attack him from behind. Two nearby rivers also helped the Athenians, as the Persian cavalry could not easily cross them.

Running the First Marathon

It was very important for the Athenians at Athens to learn of the victory. Either Pheidippides, or another runner called Eucles (*YOU-kleez*), ran the 26 miles (42 kilometers) from the battlefield to announce that the Persians had been defeated. Scarcely had he gasped out his news when he died, probably of heat exhaustion. The modern marathon race is based on his race to bring the news to Athens.

The greatest danger to the Athenian troops was that they would be surrounded by the much greater Persian forces and hacked to pieces with no possibility of escape. Greek infantry fought in lines and Miltiades decided to lengthen these lines more than normal to ensure that the Persians could not encircle them. However, there was a danger that the

This illustration, based on a seventeenth-century c.e. engraving, shows the point at which the Persians realized that they were surrounded and broke in panic, fleeing back to their ships.

longer lines would be less strong, so Miltiades placed extra troops on the wings. This made them less vulnerable to a Persian attack.

The two armies were drawn up around one mile (1.6 kilometers) apart, watching each other. The Persian troops consisted mostly of lightly armed archers who could easily be crushed by the heavily armed Greek hoplites. However, these archers had the advantage that they could fire their arrows before the Greeks could reach them. Miltiades decided that the Greeks must run the final 200 yards (180 meters) between the two forces. This way, the Greeks could tackle the archers before too many hoplites were lost. The danger with this plan was that the Greeks might lose their tight order.

The battle began with a slow advance by the Greeks, but when they started to run, the wings of the phalanx moved faster than the center, leaving the phalanx curved. When the two armies met, the Persians began to break through the center, and the Greeks there started to retreat. The Greek wings moved in toward the center, surrounding the Persian troops. The Persians

THE BATTLE OF MARATHON
—— 490 B.C.E. ——

The Battle of Marathon was a shock defeat for the Persians, who heavily outnumbered the Greeks by 25,000 to 9,000.

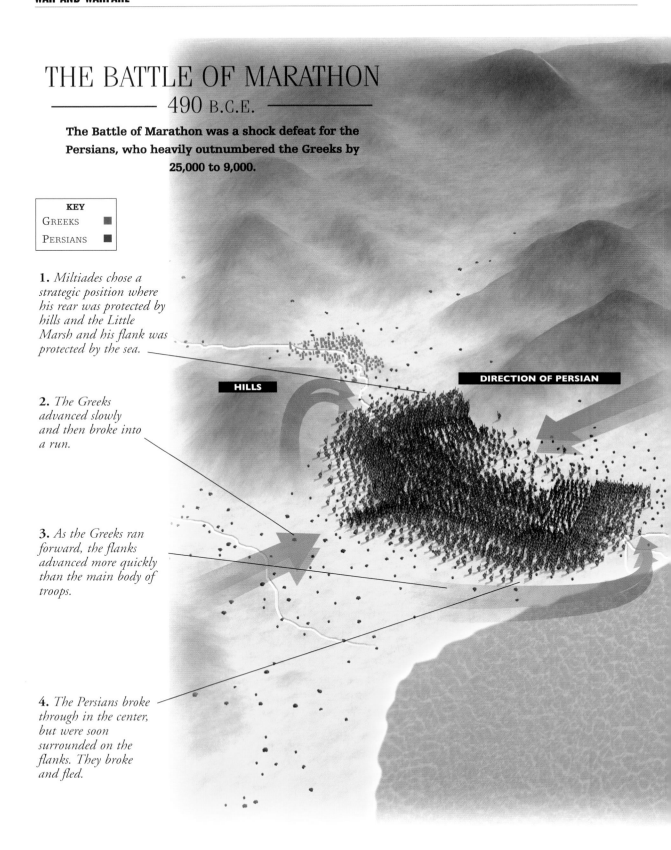

KEY
GREEKS ■
PERSIANS ■

1. *Miltiades chose a strategic position where his rear was protected by hills and the Little Marsh and his flank was protected by the sea.*

2. *The Greeks advanced slowly and then broke into a run.*

3. *As the Greeks ran forward, the flanks advanced more quickly than the main body of troops.*

4. *The Persians broke through in the center, but were soon surrounded on the flanks. They broke and fled.*

HILLS

DIRECTION OF PERSIAN

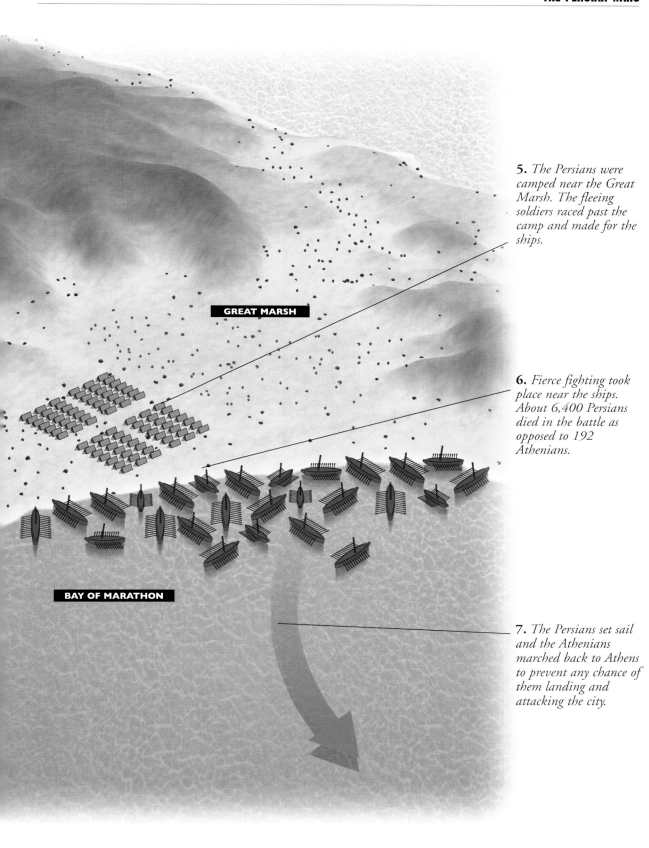

GREAT MARSH

BAY OF MARATHON

5. *The Persians were camped near the Great Marsh. The fleeing soldiers raced past the camp and made for the ships.*

6. *Fierce fighting took place near the ships. About 6,400 Persians died in the battle as opposed to 192 Athenians.*

7. *The Persians set sail and the Athenians marched back to Athens to prevent any chance of them landing and attacking the city.*

panicked and retreated toward the ships. The Greeks pursued them, cutting down many as they fled. Some 6,400 Persians were killed, but only 192 Athenians died, including their chief general, Callimachus. The Persians put to sea, but the Athenians marched back to Athens and prevented any chance of their landing. The Persians sailed back to Asia. Athens had been saved and mainland Greece was free.

The Second Invasion

Darius had no intention of letting the Greeks remain unpunished and was soon preparing for a second, much greater invasion of Greece. However, ten years passed before this invasion was launched. First, a revolt broke out in Egypt and then, in 486 B.C.E., Darius died. His son Xerxes had to make sure that his grasp of power was secure before he could afford to set out with another army. Xerxes also spent a long time preparing for the invasion.

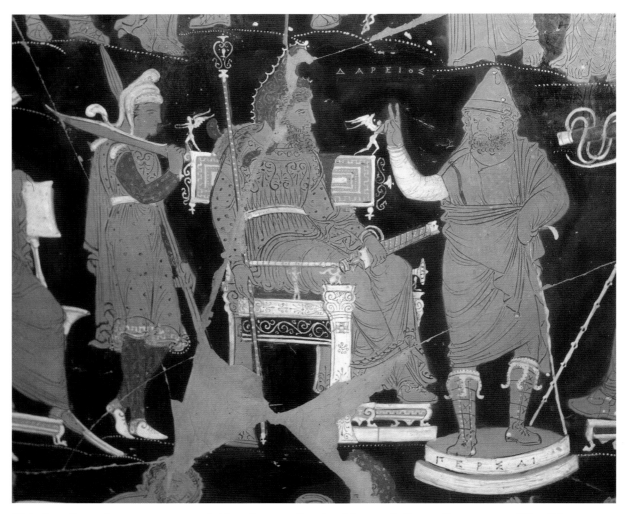

This fourth-century B.C.E. vase painting shows a Persian king seated on a throne consulting his advisors. Note how luxuriously the Persians dress in comparison to the Greeks.

Xerxes crossing the Hellespont in a painting by Jean-Adrien Guignet (1816–1854).

It is not known how many soldiers Xerxes had in his army. The historian Herodotus wrote of an army of a million men, but that is far too large a number, and the figure is probably closer to 150,000 to 250,000 warriors, backed up by non-combatants. Whatever the number, it is clear that Xerxes' army was enormous by ancient standards and greatly outnumbered the Greeks (by as much as twenty to fifty times as many men). However, size is not always a guarantee of quality. The Persian cavalry was excellent and well-trained, but the majority of the infantrymen were conscripted into the army from across the empire. Not only did many of them have no desire to serve as soldiers, but there may well have been difficulties of communication and tensions between the different tribes serving in the

Planning on a Grand Scale

Some of Xerxes' plans could only have been carried out by a king with absolute power and great wealth at his command. For example, it would be necessary to bring supplies through northern Greece, but Xerxes knew that many Persian ships had been wrecked on the Athos promontory during the first invasion of Greece. Xerxes' solution was to have a canal cut through the Athos promontory and, for three years, slaves labored to build the canal. Similarly, Xerxes wanted to be able to transport his troops and horses across the Hellespont into Europe. To use ships would take too long, so Xerxes ordered that a bridge be built. The first one consisted of ships bound together with flax and papyrus-reed ropes, but it was destroyed in a gale. Xerxes beheaded the chief engineers and ordered a second bridge. This one used stronger ropes and did last.

army. The Greeks, in contrast, were extremely well-motivated (they were defending their freedom and their way of life) and highly disciplined. The Spartans, in particular, were exceptional soldiers, as became clear at the Battle of Thermopylae.

The Battle of Thermopylae, 480 B.C.E.

In 480 B.C.E., the Persians crossed the Hellespont and marched into Greece. After some disagreement, the various Greek forces decided to attempt to stop the Persian army at Thermopylae (which means "Hot Springs"). Thermopylae was a pass which led from northern to central Greece and was very important strategically. If the Greeks failed to hold Thermopylae, there was no other easily defended pass before the Isthmus of Corinth and all mainland Greece apart from the Peloponnese would be subject to Persian domination.

The Spartan king, Leonidas, had 5,000 or 7,000 hoplites under his command, including three hundred Spartans. He was outnumbered by about forty or fifty to one. However, Thermopylae was a good place to defend because the path that snaked between the sea and the steep hills was less than 50 feet (15 meters) wide. A determined army could hold out against a larger force for a long time. Things started very promisingly for the Greeks. Every Persian attack was

Many artists and authors have been inspired by the story of Thermopylae. This idealized painting by Massimo Taparelli (1798–1866) depicts the narrow pass that was defended by Leonidas.

beaten back, leaving large numbers of dead Persians, and the Greeks still in command of the pass. Even an attack by the crack Persian troops called the Immortals was defeated. Meanwhile, a sea battle was being fought nearby at Artemisium (*Art-eh-mee-zee-um*). Two hundred Persian ships were wrecked in a storm. Greek reinforcements arrived and destroyed more ships. However, events suddenly changed course.

Although the main pass through Thermopylae was defended by the Greeks, there was a second track through the mountains, which led to a point behind the Greek position. A traitor, Ephialtes (*Eff-ee-al-teez*), revealed this track to Xerxes. Xerxes sent the Immortals up this track. There they defeated the Phoceans (*Foh-kee-ans*), who were guarding the track. The Persians could now attack the Greeks defending Thermopylae from both the front and the rear. When King Leonidas realized what had happened, he ordered all the other Greeks to leave. He would, he said, hold up the Persians for as long as possible to give his allies the chance to escape. Only a few hoplites from the nearby town of Thespiae (*THESS-pee-aye*) stayed with him. So began one of the greatest defenses in the history of war. Leonidas and his 300 Spartans took on the entire Persian army. Despite the huge disparity in numbers, the Spartans held the pass. When the Spartans' weapons were destroyed, they fought with their hands and teeth. The fighting was most intense around the figure of Leonidas. Only when he and every Spartan soldier lay dead were the Persians able to move through the pass.

Although the Greeks had been defeated, the Battle of Thermopylae proved that the Persian army was not all-powerful. A small Greek force had held them up for days and only been defeated through treachery, not superior military skill. Moreover, the battle provided huge propaganda value for the Greeks. News of the outstanding courage of the Spartan hoplites spread throughout Greece, encouraging other Greeks to join in the fight for liberty. Indeed, the actions of Leonidas and the brave 300 are still a byword for courage to this very day.

A Laconic Epitaph

The Spartans were famous for being blunt speakers who used as few words as possible. One region of Sparta is called Laconia and the English word "laconic" means a comment that is very short and to the point. The Greek writer Simonides (*Sigh-MON-i-deez*) commemorated the Spartans' bravery at Thermopylae with a short epitaph that was "laconic" both by referring to the Spartans and by being very short.

Go tell the Spartans, stranger, passing by,
That here, obedient to their laws, we lie.

The Battle of Salamis, 480 B.C.E.

The military situation was now grave. All of mainland Greece north and east of Corinth was under Persian control and only the defensive wall across the Isthmus of Corinth protected the

Peloponnese. Many Greek states were forced to accept Persian rule, but the Athenians continued to refuse to acknowledge their authority. The Delphic oracle had predicted that a wooden wall would provide safety for the Athenians. Some believed that this wall must refer to the wooden wall around the Acropolis (or high point) of Athens. Others, led by the admiral Themistocles (*The-MISS-tuh-kleez*), argued that it must mean the Athenian ships. The majority of the Athenians agreed with him, and sent their wives and children to safety on the island of Salamis. When the Persians reached Athens, they had no difficulty in capturing and burning the Acropolis and slaughtering those Athenians who remained. The wooden wall was indeed Athens' navy, which was now packed with every man who was fit to fight.

The Greek fleet consisted of ships from many different city-states, under the overall command of the Spartans. The fleet was drawn up in the straits of Salamis, around 15 miles (24 kilometers) west of Athens. However, it was heavily outnumbered, and some of the Peloponnesian city-states did not want to fight. When the Greeks saw the smoke and flames rising from the burning city of Athens, many of them thought that it was pointless to try to defend the region. However, Themistocles threatened to sail away altogether if the allies would

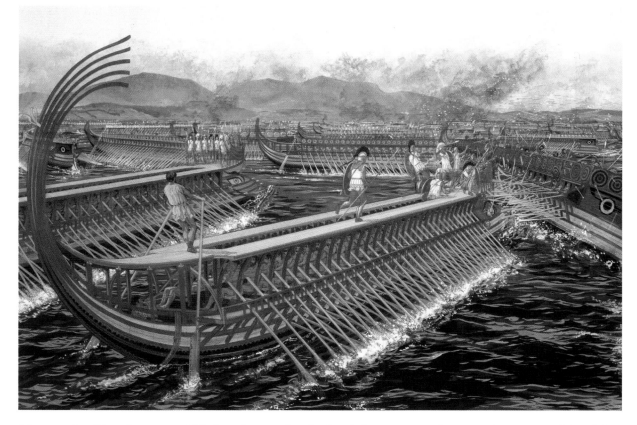

Thousands of Persians were killed at the Battle of Salamis in 480 B.C.E. The superior seamanship of the Greeks enabled them to outmaneuver the Persian ships.

not fight. The other Greeks knew that their combined fleet would be badly weakened by the loss of the Athenian ships so they reluctantly agreed with Themistocles.

Themistocles now forced the battle on his own terms. He sent one of his slaves into the Persian camp to warn Xerxes that the Greeks were going to attempt to break out from Salamis that night. Xerxes was eager for battle and believed the news. The Persian rowers sat up all night, waiting for the Greek escape attempt and were exhausted by the time daylight came. The Greeks, on the contrary, were fresh and rested. The Persians also made tactical errors. They had divided their fleet to guard every possible exit, which lessened their strength. Also, at dawn, the main body of the fleet moved into the narrowest part of the bay to intercept any fugitives, but by doing so they lost the benefit of their superior numbers. The Persians were now trapped in narrow waters without the ability to maneuver.

More Trickery by Themistocles

The Persian forces mostly consisted of conscripted men. The navy included many ships manned by Ionian Greeks who had little sympathy with the Persian cause, and did not want to fight their mainland cousins. Themistocles deliberately tried to discourage them even more. He had messages painted on the rocks near to the anchorage of the Persian fleet, asking the Ionians to desert or to fight poorly. Many did.

Xerxes was so confident of victory that he had his throne brought up to the top of a hill that looked across the strait. There he sat, expecting to see his fleet crush the Greeks. However, it was soon clear that the Persians lacked the skills of their enemy. Again and again Greeks rammed the Persian ships and sank them. Thousands of Persian sailors were drowned or speared by hoplites waiting on the shore. The Persians lost over 200 ships, but the Greeks lost only forty.

Themistocles (c. 528–462 B.C.E.) led the Greeks to victory at the Battle of Salamis. However, he fell out of favor with the Athenians and died in exile.

The Development of the Athenian Navy

In 483 B.C.E., a rich seam of silver ore was discovered in the mines at Laurion in southern Attica. Some people wanted every Athenian citizen to be given a share of the money, but the Athenian admiral, Themistocles, persuaded them to spend the money on building a fleet in readiness for war. Themistocles knew that many Athenians feared the idea of war with Persia, so he claimed that he needed the ships to attack Athens' old enemy of Aegina (*Ee-JIE-nuh*). This idea was greeted with enthusiasm, and the fleet was built.

The Battles of Plataea and Mycale, 479 B.C.E.

Xerxes was shocked at the defeat of his fleet and returned to Persia. The fleet retreated to the Hellespont, but the army was left in Greece under the leadership of Mardonius. Mardonius was an active commander and spent the spring of 479 B.C.E. ravaging Attica. The Greek troops were mostly sheltering in the Peloponnese, but eventually it was agreed that they would never get rid of the Persians until they had defeated them on land. The chosen battle site was Plataea, in central Greece. The Greeks assembled a huge army of about 30,000 hoplites with additional lightly armed troops. However, they were still outnumbered by the Persian forces. The Greeks also had no cavalry.

Initially, the Battle of Plataea went badly for the Greeks. They were under the command of the Spartan king, Pausanias (*Pow-SAY-nee-uss*), but there was considerable disagreement as to how the battle ought to be fought. Although the leaders agreed to move back closer to the town of Plataea, where there was a good supply of water, the Spartan general Amompharetus (*Am-om-FAR-eh-tuss*) refused to retreat in the face of the enemy. The Greek battle line was split and the Persians attacked, scenting an opportunity to destroy the Spartan forces. Again, the sheer professionalism of the Spartans was apparent. In vicious fighting, they managed to withstand repeated Persian attacks. Then they began their own attack. The Persian infantry was crushed, their commander Mardonius was killed, and the remaining troops broke and fled. Thousands of Persians were slaughtered or captured.

At a similar time, perhaps on the same day, the Greeks also fought the Battle of Mycale (*MIK-uh-lay*). Here, the remaining Persian ships lay at anchor. In a bold move, the Greeks landed and

600 B.C.E.		550 B.C.E.			
Archaic Period					
	550 Cyrus the Great conquers Media	546 Cyrus the Great conquers Lydia	525 Cambyses conquers Egypt	513 Darius invades Europe for the first time	

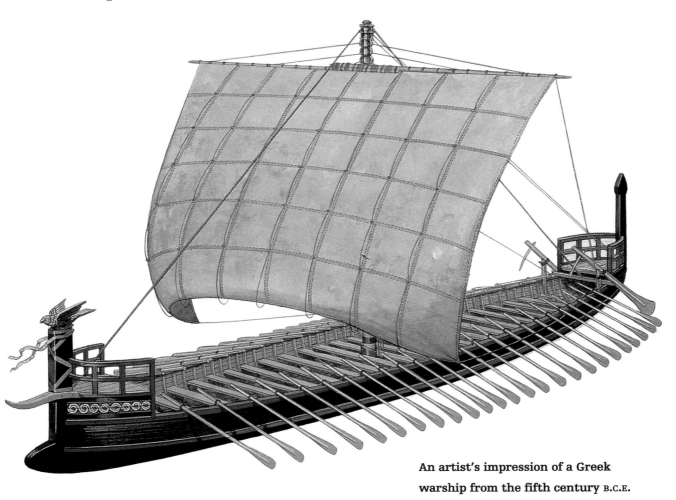

set fire to the entire fleet. Thousands were killed and the Persian fleet was destroyed. The Persians had been decisively defeated both by land and by sea. The small, divided Greek city-states had finally come together to defeat a great empire in the name of freedom. They were never to forget this success.

An artist's impression of a Greek warship from the fifth century B.C.E. The sail would have been lowered for battle.

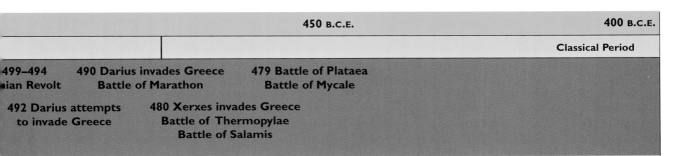

	450 B.C.E.	400 B.C.E.
		Classical Period

499–494
ian Revolt

490 Darius invades Greece
Battle of Marathon

479 Battle of Plataea
Battle of Mycale

492 Darius attempts
to invade Greece

480 Xerxes invades Greece
Battle of Thermopylae
Battle of Salamis

Chapter Three

The Peloponnesian War

During the Persian Wars, the small, quarrelsome Greek city-states had finally united to defeat an outside threat in the name of freedom. However, in the years following the Persian Wars, the Greeks showed that they were incapable of acting as a unified whole. In particular, Greece was torn apart by rivalry between Athens and Sparta, the two most important states in Greece. This rivalry was closely linked to one great political question: should the Greek states be ruled by democracies, where everyone shared power, or by oligarchies, where only a few men had power? Athens was a democracy, and Sparta was an oligarchy. As both states became increasingly powerful, it was inevitable that they would come into conflict.

The Rise of Athens: From League to Empire

At the end of the Persian Wars, there were two associations of Greek states, each led by Sparta: the Peloponnesian League, which consisted of states in southern Greece, and the Hellenic League, which consisted of many states throughout Greece. The Hellenic League had been founded to fight the Persians. However, some of the Greeks felt that the Spartans were bad leaders, and wanted to have another league to protect the Greeks from any more Persian attacks. Since Athens had contributed so much to the victory over the Persians, she was offered the leadership of this new league. The Delian (*DEE-lee-un*) League was set up in 478 B.C.E., and was named after the island of Delos, where its headquarters were located.

This vase, painted around 650–640 B.C.E., shows Greek warriors in a phalanx formation. The music of the flute player in the center helped the warriors keep in step. The Spartan army was still using flute players in the late fifth century B.C.E.

Why Some Greeks Supported Oligarchies

In the Western world today, we assume that democracy is the best form of government because every citizen has a share in power and the chance to say what they believe ought to be done. However, many Greeks believed that democracy was unstable and dangerous. They believed that ordinary people, who were often poor, were incapable of distinguishing between their own needs and the needs of the state. So, for example, ordinary people might vote to have money spent on festivals, which would help them directly, but might ignore important issues, such as the proper funding of the navy. Equally, some Greeks believed that ordinary people were too easily swayed by clever speakers into voting for bad projects. For them, democracy meant mob rule.

The Delian League achieved some notable successes, including the destruction of the Persian fleet at the Battle of Eurymedon (*You-RIM-e-don*) in 469 B.C.E. Piracy was reduced, trade improved, and the Ionian Greeks remained free, although Persia still maintained control over Cyprus. However, the Athenians gradually gained increasing power over the league. League states were expected to provide a certain number of warships each year or to contribute money to cover their costs. Most league members chose to pay money, which was easier for them, but this left Athens as the state with the strongest navy. Garrisons of Athenian troops were often present in allied cities and the Athenian fleet patrolled the Aegean Sea. Allied states no longer had a vote

Delos as it is today. The island was the headquarters of the Delian League until 454 B.C.E., when it moved to Athens.

in league meetings, and any state that rebelled and left the league was punished harshly. When the island of Thasos (*THAY-soss*) revolted in 465 B.C.E., the Athenians crushed this revolt and treated Thasos as a conquered enemy. Thasos lost her fleet, her city walls, and her independence. In 454 B.C.E., the Athenians moved the league treasury from Delos to Athens, thus ensuring that they had complete control over the league finances. By the 440s B.C.E., there were over 200 city-states allied to Athens, and she was increasingly ready to reveal her dominance over the Delian League. What had started as a league of free Greeks to punish the Persians had, in fact, become an Athenian Empire.

For many Greeks, rule by democratic Athens, relative peace, increased trade, and the suppression of piracy may have outweighed the fact that their city-states had lost their freedom to act as they pleased. However, there were many states that were becoming resentful of Athenian domination of their affairs and readily supported Sparta when she promised to free them from Athenian tyranny.

The Outbreak of War, 431 B.C.E.

From the 470s B.C.E. onward, Sparta and Athens became increasingly hostile. Matters worsened when an Athenian force, which had been sent to help Sparta crush a revolt by the Helots, was asked to return home. The Athenians were deeply offended at this snub and existing tensions between the two states boiled over. For much of the 450s and 440s B.C.E. Sparta and Athens were at war, but in 446 B.C.E. peace was agreed on between the two sides. However, it was not to last.

Sparta could see that Athens was becoming very powerful, and feared that she would be overtaken as the most important Greek state. Moreover, the Spartans did not like democracy. Athens supported democracy throughout her empire, and Sparta regarded this as yet another threat. She did not want the idea of democracy to spread to the regions she controlled. If democracy spread too far, the entire basis of Spartan life would be threatened.

Moreover, Athens was expanding her power westward, a matter of considerable concern to the state of Corinth, which had many colonies in that area. Corinth was an important ally of Sparta, and demanded that Sparta support her against Athens. As the Corinthians pointed out, the Spartan alliance was meant to provide allies with protection from outside threats. If Sparta could not do so, then Corinth stated that she would leave the Spartan alliance. This was a very serious threat for Sparta. If Corinth left, not only would Sparta lose the use of Corinth's powerful navy, but also many other Spartan allies would be tempted to break away. The Peloponnesian League could fall apart and Sparta might be left isolated. Sparta demanded that Athens free the members of the Delian League from Athenian influence. This effectively meant an end to the Athenian Empire. The Athenians, never intending to give up their political power, countered with a similar demand regarding the Peloponnesian League. Neither side

The Parthenon at Athens was just one of the buildings that were paid for with money from the Athenian Empire.

Pericles—The Architect of Empire

Pericles (c. 495–429 B.C.E.) was an outstanding orator and politician who dominated Athenian politics during the mid-fifth century B.C.E. He was elected as general every year for fifteen years until he died of plague. Pericles was a great imperialist. He wanted to see the Athenian Empire expand and supported colonization in various parts of the Greek world. He believed that the Athenian Empire protected the weak from oppression. He was also a democrat and believed in people having the freedom to do what they wanted in private, as long as they obeyed the law in public matters. Pericles was not only an active politician, but also a great admirer of beautiful things. He ensured that some of the tribute paid by the members of the Athenian Empire was spent on rebuilding the Athenian Acropolis. The Acropolis had been sacked by the Persians in 480 B.C.E. and it was essential that the temples to the gods be rebuilt. Pericles drove forward much of the building program, and it was during this time that the Parthenon and other fine temples were erected on the Acropolis.

would back down. War was declared. The stage was now set for an increasingly violent struggle which engulfed the Greek world for well over twenty years.

The Early War Years, 431–421 B.C.E.

Sparta was a land-based power with a professional infantry, but no effective navy. Athens had the largest navy in Greece, but was much weaker on land. Therefore, the two states had very different strategies. Sparta could not defeat Athens at sea, which was the basis of Athenian power, so she struck at the heart of the empire, Athens herself. Every year, Sparta sent troops into Athenian territory to ravage the land. The intention was that Athens would be forced to surrender when she ran out of supplies. However, the Athenian general, Pericles (*PERRY-kleez*), had foreseen this strategy and had ordered all the inhabitants of the countryside to be evacuated into the city, where they could shelter behind the Long Walls. The Long Walls stretched down from the city to the sea and prevented Athens from being besieged.

The Athenian statesman, Pericles, lived from around 495–429 B.C.E. He supported the increase in Athenian power in the mid-fifth century B.C.E.

The Plague, 430 B.C.E.

Modern scientists are not sure what the plague was. It may have been typhus, measles, or pneumonic plague. However, it is clear from the descriptions of it that it was an extremely unpleasant illness. In this extract from Thucydides' *History of the Peloponnesian War*, he describes some of the symptoms:

First there was a burning sensation in the head, accompanied by inflammation of the eyes, bleeding of the throat and tongue, and foul breath. Then sneezing and hoarseness of the voice set in and in a short time the pain moved down to the chest. At this point there was also severe coughing. Then the stomach was upset and all kinds of bile was vomited up in great pain. The skin broke out in small blisters and ulcers. Patients felt as if they were burning up *inside and suffered from unquenchable thirst. The majority died from this fever on the seventh or eighth day. If they survived, then the disease went down into the bowels where it caused both violent ulceration and acute diarrhoea at the same time. Most of the remaining victims of the disease died owing to weakness caused by the diarrhoea.*

Thucydides

The plague caused terrible suffering at Athens and about one-third of the population died.

While Athens had her navy, she had no difficulty in importing supplies. Pericles ordered that the Athenians avoid pitched battles with the Spartans to avert possible defeat. (Pericles was correct—the only battle that Athens fought on land at this point was lost.) Instead, the Athenians were to use the power of their ships to sail around the Peloponnese, launching raids on Sparta and her allies, thus interrupting trade and damaging their lands. Pericles believed that this policy would wear down the Spartans and the Peloponnesians over time, but that Athenian interests would not be badly damaged.

In the beginning, Pericles' policy was successful. Although country dwellers found it distressing to know that their fields were being ruined by the Spartan troops, there was no lack of money to look after them inside Athens. Athens also had the satisfaction of launching successful raids on the Peloponnese. Then disaster struck. A highly infectious plague spread through Athens between 430 and 427 B.C.E., killing about one-third of the population. The great number of people who had come into the city from the countryside helped the plague to spread rapidly. There was severe loss of life, and morale plummeted. Prayers had no effect and doctors were unable to cure the disease. Law-abiding citizens, who had always respected the gods, died just as commonly as those who were dishonest or who had failed to honor the gods. Even Pericles, the great leader of Athens, died. Society began to break down under the strain—the sick were not nursed, bodies lay unburied, people lost faith in the gods and the laws. When anybody might be struck down without warning, people lost all restraint and lived for pleasure alone.

Shocked at the effects of the plague, Athens sought peace with Sparta in 430 B.C.E. However, this was rejected and war continued. By this stage, the war was becoming increasingly vicious. In the summer of 429 B.C.E., the Spartans besieged Plataea, which had done so much to help the Greek cause in the Persian Wars. Plataea held out for two years until the starving inhabitants surrendered. The Spartans asked each captive what they had done to help Sparta in the current war. Naturally, Athens' close allies would not have helped Sparta, but this point did not save them. As each man replied that he had done nothing to help Sparta he was taken off and killed. The women and children were then enslaved.

In 427 B.C.E., civil war broke out at Corcyra (*COR-sy-rah*). It was an indication of what was to come in many Greek states as democrats and oligarchs struggled for supremacy. When the democrats gained control, they took the opportunity to take revenge on the oligarchs. They had no hesitation in twisting the meaning of words. Anyone who argued for moderation was called a coward. Vengeance became more important than innocence, and the desire to get rich overruled all ideas of justice. People were condemned to death, not because of any crime on their part, but because a democrat wanted to seize their property. Political ties proved to be stronger than family loyalty, and fathers were ready to kill their sons for supporting the wrong political side.

A Daring Raid into Spartan Territory

In 425 B.C.E., the Athenians achieved a remarkable success. The general Demosthenes (*Dem-OSS-thuh-neez*, no relation to the fourth-century orator of the same name) decided to take the war deep into Spartan territory by establishing a base in the southern Peloponnese. He sailed to Pylos (*PI-loss*) and built a small fort on the mainland, about 45 miles (72 kilometers) from Sparta. From there he intended to launch raids into Spartan territory and stir up trouble among the Helots, who hated acting as slaves for the Spartans. When the Spartans learned of Demosthenes' actions, they immediately withdrew from Attica and marched home. They decided to place a party of hoplites on an island opposite Pylos, called Sphacteria (*Sfak-TEE-ree-uh*). They also attacked the fort at Pylos with their ships. However, things went very wrong for the Spartans.

First, the Athenian fleet turned up and defeated the Spartan ships. Thus, the Spartans on the island were cut off and the Athenian fleet prevented them from escaping. The Spartans offered peace terms to the Athenians. It looked as if Pericles' policy of attrition had worked. However, the Athenians rejected the offer of peace, and war resumed. Eventually, the Athenians landed a group of soldiers on the island, who fought their way toward the Spartans. Finally, the Spartan forces surrendered, including over 200 Spartan hoplites. True Spartans were never supposed to be captured, but die in battle. However, these hoplites were now held hostage by the Athenians. The Spartan state had been publicly shamed. Moreover, it could not afford to lose so many trained soldiers.

Sparta realized that her attempt to break Athens by ravaging her land was not going to work, particularly when the Athenians threatened to kill the hostages if the Spartans were to enter Attica again. The only way they could defeat Athens would be to cut off her source of wealth. If Athens' allies were attacked, they would no longer pay her tribute. Without tribute, Athens would be in no position to continue the war. Sparta therefore launched a campaign into northern Greece under their able general Brasidas (*BRAS-ee-dass*). Brasidas managed to win over many of the Greek states in the region. However, as the Spartans made progress in

Athens Builds Her Empire During the Peace

Athens took advantage of the break in open warfare to try to increase her power. One attempt concerned the island of Melos (*MEE-loss*). Melos had been neutral throughout the Peloponnesian War and was the only island in the southern Aegean Sea which was not under Athenian control. Athens demanded that Melos become part of the Athenian Empire or be destroyed. The inhabitants argued that this was an unjust demand and that they wanted to stay neutral as before. Athens ignored the argument that the Melians had not helped the Spartans in the war. The fact that they had not been on Athens' side was enough. Athens attacked Melos, killed the men, and enslaved the women and children.

northern Greece, they were troubled by events in the south: a treaty with Argos, their chief enemy in the Peloponnese, was coming to an end, they feared that their Helot slaves might revolt, and they still desperately needed to secure the release of their hoplites. Therefore, in 421 B.C.E., they again proposed peace. This time, the Athenians accepted.

War Resumes

Although Sparta and Athens made peace in 421 B.C.E., it did not last. Many of Sparta's allies were unhappy that she had not crushed Athens. Corinth tried to build up an alliance of Peloponnesian states that did not accept the peace. Although Sparta managed to prevent this, it was clear that the peace was not seen as a long-term settlement, but rather a breathing space in a longer war. On the Athenian side, too, there was a sense that the war was on hold, rather than over. Athens became an ally of Argos, Sparta's old enemy. When the combined Argive and Athenian army attacked the small state of Tegea (*Tuh-JEE-uh*) in 418 B.C.E., the Spartans defeated them at the Battle of Mantinea (*Man-tin-EE-uh*). Technically, this was not a breach of the peace treaty as neither side was attacking the other's territory. However, it was clear that Athens and Sparta remained hostile. Finally, in 414 B.C.E., the Athenians carried out a raid on Spartan territory. This was clearly against the peace terms and the Spartans had no hesitation in asking for arbitration of their dispute. The Athenians refused, and war resumed in 413 B.C.E.

The citizens of Syracuse were avid followers of the theater. Their love of drama led them to free some captured Athenians who could recite parts of Euripides' plays.

The Sicilian Expedition

Pericles had urged the Athenians not to try to extend their power too far. He believed that the navy should be used for guarding the Athenian Empire or raiding Sparta. It should not be used to expand the empire outside its natural boundaries of the Aegean Sea and some parts of northern Greece. However, when Athens received an appeal from her ally, Egesta (*E-GUESS-tuh*), on the island of Sicily, the warning against over-expansion was ignored, with disastrous consequences.

Egesta was at war with another Sicilian state, Selinous (*Sel-EE-noos*). Selinous had gained the support of the powerful democratic state of Syracuse, so Egesta desperately needed similar backing. Egesta claimed to be able to pay for the war and, in 415 B.C.E., the Athenians agreed to send sixty ships to help her. They wanted to help an ally, and to bring much of Sicily into the Athenian Empire. However, the Athenians had greatly miscalculated the relative strengths of Egesta and Syracuse. Egesta was not as wealthy as she had claimed, whereas Syracuse was rich, well-armed, and well-led. In contrast, the Athenians were campaigning far from home, which made it difficult to react to events or to bring in supplies and reinforcements. Moreover, the Syracusans had an excellent navy, easily able to take on the Athenians. Above all, the Sicilian expedition suffered from poor leadership. The Athenians had sent three generals to command the expedition, each with different views on how to fight Syracuse. Alcibiades was a brilliant leader, but was recalled to face trial, having been accused of sacrilege—disrespect toward something considered sacred—in the middle of the expedition. Nicias (*NICK-ee-uss*) had not voted for the

The Peloponnesian War was soon to spread to Sicily, when the Athenians decided to attack Selinous and her ally, Syracuse. This photograph shows the ruins of one of the temples at Selinous.

Alcibiades: Traitor or Wronged Man?

Alcibiades (*Al-see-BYE-uh-deez*) lived from around 450 to 404 B.C.E. He was a brilliant, charming, charismatic man who was both loved and hated in Athens. He was a relative of Pericles and was brought up in his household. He was a pupil and friend of the philosopher Socrates. Alcibiades was a strong believer in Athenian expansion, hence his support for the Sicilian expedition. When he was recalled to Athens by his political enemies to face trial for sacrilege, he managed to escape. He knew that he would probably be condemned to death, so he fled to Sparta. Even though Sparta was at war with Athens, he gave the Spartans military advice on how to defeat Athens (such as sending troops to Sicily and fortifying a base in Attica for all-year raiding expeditions).

In 412 B.C.E., Alcibiades went to Ionia, where he stirred up revolts among members of the Athenian Empire. Eventually, he became unpopular with the Spartans, who did not trust him. He fled to the Persian governor of Ionia, where he worked to help Athens. The Athenians appointed Alcibiades commander of the Ionian fleet in 407 B.C.E.

He led the fleet brilliantly, but it was defeated while he was away on a diplomatic mission. Knowing that he would be held responsible, he refused to return to Athens, but retired to his estate in Thrace. In 405 B.C.E., he warned the Athenians about the Persian threat to their fleet. They ignored him and lost the final sea battle of the war. This was the end of Alcibiades' influence. There was no role for him in Athens, he was distrusted by the Spartans, and only the Persians were prepared to give him sanctuary. However, even this was not to last. In 404 B.C.E. the Spartan general, Lysander, persuaded the Persians to murder him.

Alcibiades had a reputation for brilliance, but he ended up telling Athens' enemies how to defeat her.

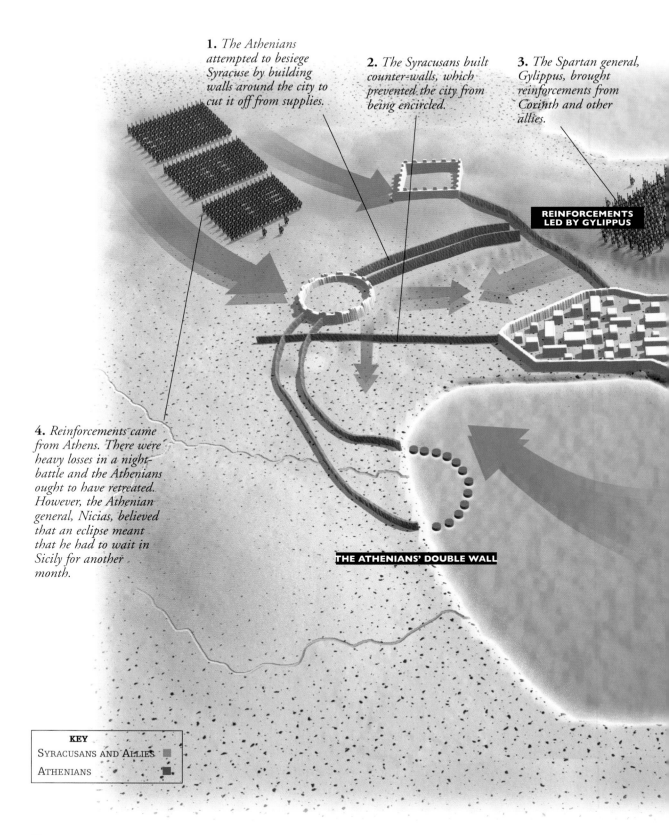

1. The Athenians attempted to besiege Syracuse by building walls around the city to cut it off from supplies.

2. The Syracusans built counter-walls, which prevented the city from being encircled.

3. The Spartan general, Gylippus, brought reinforcements from Corinth and other allies.

REINFORCEMENTS LED BY GYLIPPUS

4. Reinforcements came from Athens. There were heavy losses in a night-battle and the Athenians ought to have retreated. However, the Athenian general, Nicias, believed that an eclipse meant that he had to wait in Sicily for another month.

THE ATHENIANS' DOUBLE WALL

KEY

Syracusans and Allies ■

Athenians ■

SIEGE OF SYRACUSE
———— 414–413 B.C.E. ————

The siege of Syracuse ended in disaster for the Athenians.

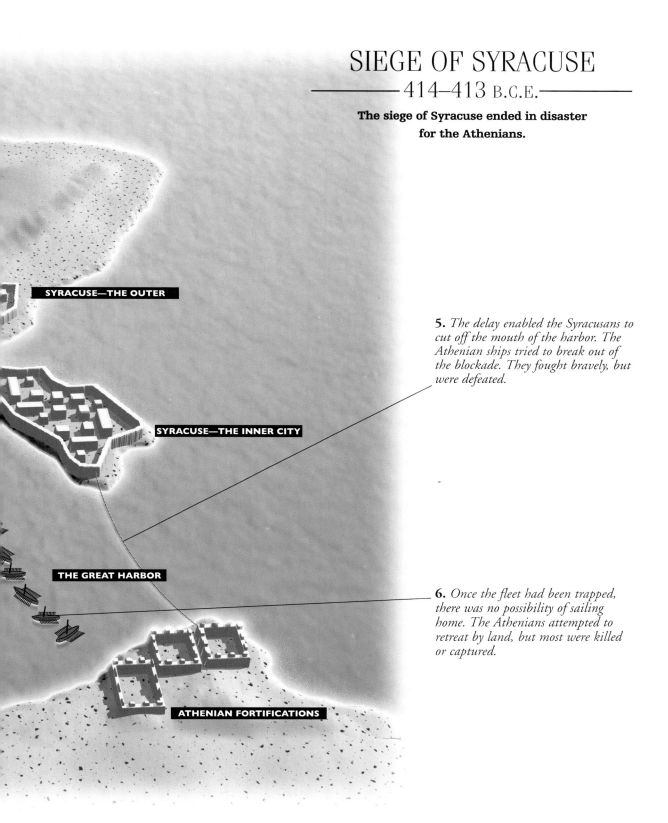

SYRACUSE—THE OUTER

SYRACUSE—THE INNER CITY

THE GREAT HARBOR

ATHENIAN FORTIFICATIONS

5. *The delay enabled the Syracusans to cut off the mouth of the harbor. The Athenian ships tried to break out of the blockade. They fought bravely, but were defeated.*

6. *Once the fleet had been trapped, there was no possibility of sailing home. The Athenians attempted to retreat by land, but most were killed or captured.*

expedition and did not believe that it could succeed. The third general, Lamachus (*LAM-uh-kuss*), was an experienced soldier who supported the expedition. However, he was killed in 414 B.C.E. The leadership of the Sicilian expedition now fell to Nicias, a man who expected defeat.

The Spartans sent Gylippus (*GUY-lip-us*) to advise the Syracusans. Before long, he was able to undermine all the initial Athenian successes. Soon it became clear that the situation was unsafe. Nicias sent a letter to Athens begging for help—either he must leave Sicily or reinforcements must be sent out under a new commander. Reinforcements came, led by Demosthenes, who had led the successful raid on Pylos. Demosthenes urged Nicias to leave Sicily before it was too late, but Nicias was old, ill, and superstitious. Just when Demosthenes had persuaded him to leave, there was an eclipse of the moon. Soothsayers told Nicias that he must not leave until one month had passed. However, this delay gave the Syracusans time to trap the Athenians in the Great Harbor at Syracuse. When the Athenians tried to break out it was too late. With the fleet defeated, the land forces were trapped on Sicily without any means of escape. Thousands were killed, and thousands more were captured and sent to work in the Sicilian quarries. Only a few survived, having been granted their freedom because they could recite extracts from the poet Euripides' (*You-RIP-i-deez*) plays. However, most of Athens' great force of ships had been destroyed and most of her army lay dead on the battlefields. This was a blow from which she could not recover.

The Final Years of War, 412–404 B.C.E.

After the disaster in Sicily, Athens was greatly weakened both in morale and in manpower. Her enormous losses had crippled her war effort. Many of her allies had revolted and the Spartans constantly pursued an aggressive policy of attacking Athenian land. They fortified Decelea (*DECK-uh-lay-uh*) and used it as a launch point for regular attacks on Attica. Slaves fled in thousands and the fields yielded nothing for those cooped up in Athens. Athens was completely dependent on the corn ships, which continued to arrive from the Hellespont and Black Sea regions. However, Sparta now had a means of interrupting this supply of food. Persia and Sparta had made an alliance in 411 B.C.E., which left the Persians in control of the Ionian Greeks. In return Persia, who wanted to see Athens defeated, provided Sparta with a fleet.

480 B.C.E.		460 B.C.E.	
Classical Period			
478 Delian League set up	469 Battle of Eurymedon Persian fleet destroyed		454 Delian League treasury moved to Athens

Although the Athenians won some naval victories, such as those at Cyzicus (*SID-zee-kuss*) in 410 B.C.E. and Arginusae (*Arg-in-OO-sigh*) in 406 B.C.E., it was increasingly difficult to find the resources to build ships to replace losses.

In 405 B.C.E., Athenian naval power was shattered when the Spartan general Lysander defeated the Athenians at the Battle of Aegospotamoi (*Ay-gos-POT-am-oi*). Without a good fleet, Athens was cut off from the outside world by land and sea. The grain fleets no longer came, and soon starvation stalked the city. Athens was finally forced to admit defeat. Sparta's allies demanded the destruction of the city, but the Spartans argued that Athens had achieved too much in the Persian Wars to be destroyed. Even so, Sparta's terms made it clear that Athens' dominance was at an end. The Long Walls and other fortifications were torn down, her navy was restricted to twelve ships, and she was to be ruled by an oligarchy. For the moment, the Athenian Empire was finished. Athens was now an ally of Sparta and subject to her rule.

The harbor at Syracuse today retains much the same shape as it had in 415 B.C.E.

	420 B.C.E.		400 B.C.E.
431 War declared between Sparta and Athens	425 Spartans captured at Sphacteria	418 Battle of Mantinea	405 Battle of Aegospotamoi
430–427 Plague in Athens	421 Peace treaty agreed	415–413 Sicilian Expedition	404 Athens defeated
431–429 Siege of Plataea			

Chapter Four

Alexander the Great

After the end of the Peloponnesian War, the Greek states were worn out by years of violent conflict. In particular, the two leading states, Athens and Sparta, were no longer as powerful as they had been. Athens had been defeated in the Peloponnesian War and had lost her empire, which had been a source of great wealth and power. Although she continued to be an important state, she was nowhere near as powerful as she had been in the fifth century. Sparta had won the Peloponnesian War and, for a time, became the most important state in Greece. However, she had lost many of her citizens in the war and did not have the money or the manpower to support an army throughout the whole of Greece and Ionia. Moreover, other states in Greece were increasing in power and resented her rule.

The final blow for Sparta came with the rise of Thebes (*THEE-bzz*). Thebes was the leading state in Boeotia (*Bee-OH-she-uh*), in central Greece. Boeotia had some of the richest agricultural land in Greece. This agricultural wealth enabled Thebes to develop strong cavalry forces. The Boeotian states disliked Sparta's attempts to dictate how they were ruled and supported Thebes when she challenged Sparta in war. Thebes inflicted a crushing defeat on the Spartans at the Battle of Leuctra (*LOOK-truh*) in 371 B.C.E. This battle sent shock waves throughout Greece. The previously invincible Spartan infantry had been decisively beaten. Thebes followed up this battle the next year by invading Sparta and setting free the Helots of Messenia

This modern illustration shows Alexander the Great fighting at the Battle of Granicus River in 334 B.C.E. The Persians were drawn up on the opposite bank and Alexander was forced to lead his army across the river in order to attack them.

(*Mess-EE-nee-uh*). Thus Sparta no longer had a nation of slaves to produce her food. Instead, there was a powerful state on her borders, inhabited by former slaves who loathed the Spartans. Sparta now had to protect herself from possible attack, rather than taking part in foreign adventures.

The Rise of Macedon and Philip II

In the 350s B.C.E., there was another shift in the balance of power. Most Greeks regarded Macedon, in the far north of Greece, as so far away and strange that it was not really Greek at all. However, in 359 B.C.E., Macedon had a new king, Philip II, who was an exceptional organizer. He united the warring tribes of Macedon and created a formidable professional army. Backed by this, he proceeded to expand his power.

Athens strongly opposed the increasing influence of Macedon. The orator Demosthenes argued that it was essential that all the Greek city-states unite and defeat Macedon, but the Greeks were too

Did Alexander Kill His Father?

It is not known why Philip was killed, and Alexander cut down the assassin before he could be interrogated. However, even in ancient times, there was some suspicion that Alexander may have been involved. In Macedon, eldest sons did not automatically become king. Moreover, Philip disliked Alexander's mother, Olympias (*O-LIM-pee-uss*), and had remarried. Had Philip lived for several more years Alexander might not have become king. Alexander was ruthless and ambitious and, in later life, killed some of his friends. Perhaps he rated having power as more important than having a father?

A gold coin showing the head of Philip II of Macedon.

disorganized for this approach to work. Instead, Philip picked off each city-state individually. Some were won over with promises of alliance. Others were defeated in war or yielded when a Macedonian army appeared on their borders. Eventually, Athens, Thebes, and the Theban allies decided to fight Philip in battle. After a crushing defeat at the Battle of Chaeronea (*Kai-ROH-nee-uh*) in 338 B.C.E., all of Greece was under Macedonian control. In 337 B.C.E., Philip proposed the invasion of Persia, gathering together a large army of Macedonians and other Greeks.

Philip had long planned to invade the Persian Empire. He claimed that this was partly to liberate the Ionian Greeks and partly to punish the Persians for having invaded Greece during the Persian Wars. However, this was mostly propaganda. The reality was that Persia was a very rich land on the borders of the Greek world. The Greeks were poor and Persia offered opportunities for untold wealth and the expansion of Greek power. However, when all the preparations were ready for the invasion, Philip was assassinated. His twenty-year-old son, Alexander, inherited his throne.

The Story of Bucephalus

One day, horse traders were trying to sell Philip a magnificent stallion. However, the horse refused to obey anyone and appeared to be impossible to ride. Alexander was watching and said that the riders should not be so clumsy. Philip was angry with Alexander and asked him whether he thought he could ride it any better. Alexander soon proved that he could. He had noticed that the horse was frightened of its shadow, so he turned it to face the sun and soothed it. Then he mounted the horse and rode it. Philip commented that Macedon was clearly too small to contain Alexander's talent and that he would need to find a kingdom big enough for him. Alexander named the horse Bucephalus (*Bu-KEFF-uh-luss*), or Ox-Head, because of the size of its head.

This carving shows Alexander on horseback. Alexander was a notable rider and often rode into battle at the head of his troops.

Alexander the Great

Alexander was born in 356 B.C.E. He was educated by the philosopher Aristotle, and showed signs of considerable ability at an early age. When Alexander was sixteen, Philip chose him to act as his deputy. At eighteen, he led the left wing of the Macedonian cavalry in the Battle of Chaeronea. This was an important command and he did well in it, breaking through Greek lines and helping to achieve victory. When Philip was assassinated in 336 B.C.E. Alexander became king. At the age of only twenty he was in charge of Macedon and, two years later, the invasion of Persia.

The Invasion of Persia

In 338 B.C.E., the king of Persia was murdered. For three years various rivals tried to seize the throne until, finally, Darius III became king. He had control of a vast empire and resources that completely outstripped those of Greece. Alexander's army was quite small, with 30,000 infantry (12,000 of whom were Macedonian) and 5,000 cavalry (1,800 of whom were Macedonian). In contrast, Darius commanded over 100,000 soldiers. However, Persian troops tended to be recruited from across the empire, rather than solely from the region of Persia. This meant that the troops often had no strong loyalty to the Persian king. For example, much of Darius' naval force of 400 ships came from Egypt. Egypt had a long history of conflict with Persia, and Egyptian troops were often unreliable in battle. The Persian forces were also not very strong. Darius' best troops were his cavalry, particularly the 2,000 permanent King's Bodyguard. However, the infantry was disorganized and poorly trained and equipped. To make the infantry stronger, Persian commanders tended to recruit Greek mercenaries. Darius had about 30,000 mercenaries, so it was inevitable that Greeks would fight against other Greeks during the invasion.

The Battle of Granicus River, 334 B.C.E.

The first battle of the invasion was the Battle of Granicus River (*GRAN-i-kuss*), where the Persians had a strong defensive position. However, while the Persians outnumbered Alexander in cavalry (around 10,000 to 5,000), Alexander had significantly more infantry (around 13,000 as opposed to 5,000 mercenaries). Moreover, Alexander had no choice but to meet the Persians in battle. If he did not fight the Persians, but avoided their position, he would have a strong Persian force behind him. They would have been able to harass him and cut off supplies as he marched further into the empire.

The Battle of Granicus River in May 334 B.C.E. is shown in an oil painting by the Venetian artist Francesco Fontebasso (1707–1769).

Alexander's forces crossed the river and attacked the Persian left wing with a joint assault by his cavalry and infantry. The Persian cavalry were drawn away from their position and lost their formation. Alexander's infantry were then able to break through the Persian line, killing thousands. The Greek mercenaries in the pay of Darius were caught on the plain and massacred. About 3,000 died and others were taken prisoner.

Darius was not present at this battle. The commanders were the local satraps (or governors) and noblemen. Great numbers of them were killed in the battle and the death rate damaged Persian organization. However, although Alexander had won an important victory, he still had to face the main Persian army.

Before attempting to defeat the Persians again in battle, Alexander took time to consolidate his hold over the coastal parts of Asia Minor (in modern Turkey). He allowed the Greek city-states to use their own laws and freed them from paying taxes to Persia. He also set up democracies in many of the towns and claimed that he was fighting to free the Greek city-states from Persian control. This was excellent propaganda, both locally and back in mainland Greece, where many still resented his conquest of Greece.

The Battle of Issus, 333 B.C.E.

Alexander now moved south and met the Persians at Issus (in modern Syria). The scene of the battle was a small plain about 1.5 miles (2.4 kilometers) wide, lying between the mountains and the sea. Alexander's troops were drawn up facing the Persians with the mountains to their right and the sea to their left. The Macedonian phalanx was in the center of the Greek battle line and Alexander was on the right of the phalanx with the elite Macedonian troops, the infantry Guards and the Companion cavalry. On the left, Alexander had placed his allied cavalry and his weaker forces. Darius was positioned in the center of the Persian battle line, flanked by groups of Greek hoplite mercenaries. The wings consisted of Persian infantry with archers in front of them. The Persian cavalry was placed on the right wing.

Both Alexander and the Persians were strongest on their right wings. Alexander's plan was to attack the Persian left wing and to thrust forward to try to reach Darius. By leaving his weaker troops to face the Persian

The Destruction of Thebes

In 335 B.C.E., there was a rumor that Alexander had died. The Thebans, who resented being ruled by Macedon, revolted and besieged the Macedonian garrison. Alexander marched 300 miles (480 kilometers) in thirteen days and attacked Thebes. After it was captured, it was razed to the ground and the inhabitants were sold into slavery. To see a once powerful state treated in this way was shocking for the other Greek states and showed the ruthlessness of the young Macedonian king.

This Roman mosaic was copied from an original Greek painting and shows Alexander at the heart of the Battle of Issus, pursuing the Persian king, Darius III.

cavalry, he was risking the Persian cavalry breaking through and attacking the Macedonian phalanx. However, he thought this risk worthwhile because it meant he could use his strongest troops to break the Persian infantry. Although he had to send a detachment of Thessalian cavalry to reinforce his left wing, Alexander's plan worked. The Persian infantry were defeated and as Alexander fought his way toward Darius, the Persian king's nerve broke and he fled. Seeing their king in headlong flight, the rest of the Persians ran for safety. Thousands were killed in the pursuit, and the royal family was captured, including the king's mother, wife, and daughters. Darius fled from the battle to the center of his empire, near the Euphrates River. There he tried to make peace with Alexander, but Alexander refused any offer of alliance with Darius, stating that he was now the "Lord of Asia" and the true king.

Alexander's fleet was not strong enough to defeat the Persians in outright battle, so he decided to cut off the Persians from the Mediterranean. His army made its way through Syria capturing important coastal towns. The best defended city was Tyre, which held out under siege for six months in 332 B.C.E. Although the long siege delayed Alexander more than he had expected, he had no choice but to remain and capture the city. If he had not, he would have had a powerful enemy state to his rear, threatening his line of communication. Moreover, by taking Tyre, he had shattered the power of the Persian fleet.

After Tyre fell, the road to Egypt lay open. Egypt was a rich state that had always resented Persian rule. Alexander respected the local gods and was happy to sacrifice to them. This impressed the Egyptians, and they believed that Alexander offered the chance of better rule. Alexander soon gained control of Egypt, which provided him with good food supplies and a fleet.

The Battle of Gaugamela, 331 B.C.E.

With Egypt under control, Alexander could deal with the eastern sections of the Persian Empire. Moreover, he knew that he had to defeat Darius. Before long, the two armies met at Gaugamela (*GOW-guh-mell-uh*) in Babylonia. The Persians greatly outnumbered Alexander, perhaps by five to one, particularly in cavalry. They were also positioned on an open plain, which would be very favorable to cavalry, and allowed Darius to use his 200 war chariots. However, the Persians were weak in terms of infantry, with poor-quality troops recruited from across the empire, who lacked good weapons and sufficient training.

Alexander knew that his main threat was that he might be outflanked. Therefore, he took two precautions. He placed a group of Guards on each wing to protect against attacks on his flanks. He also created a reserve phalanx to his rear so that, if he were outflanked, the reserve phalanx could move up and protect the rear of the main army. The front line of the army consisted of the Companions, Alexander, and the Guards on the right, the Macedonian phalanx in the middle, and the Thessalian cavalry on the left.

The Persians had drawn up their army in two lines. The weaker infantry was placed behind the stronger troops. Darius was in the middle of the Persian line, flanked by his horseguards. On either side of these were Greek mercenary hoplites. Heavy cavalry were positioned on either flank. In front of the main Persian battle line were the war chariots.

The battle started with an attack by the war chariots. However, the well-trained Macedonian phalanx maneuvered to open gaps in its ranks. The chariots could not respond in time and drove through the gaps. As they stopped in order to turn around, the Macedonians fell on them and massacred them.

Alexander greatly admired mythical Greek heroes. His portrait was deliberately cast in a heroic mold.

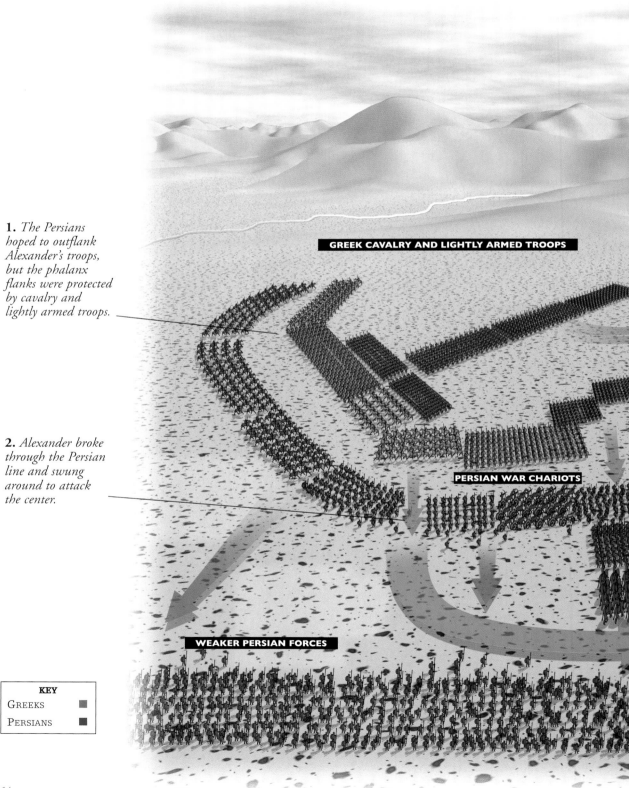

1. *The Persians hoped to outflank Alexander's troops, but the phalanx flanks were protected by cavalry and lightly armed troops.*

2. *Alexander broke through the Persian line and swung around to attack the center.*

GREEK CAVALRY AND LIGHTLY ARMED TROOPS

PERSIAN WAR CHARIOTS

WEAKER PERSIAN FORCES

KEY	
GREEKS	■
PERSIANS	■

THE BATTLE OF GAUGAMELA
331 B.C.E.

Alexander won this decisive battle, despite being outnumbered by about five to one.

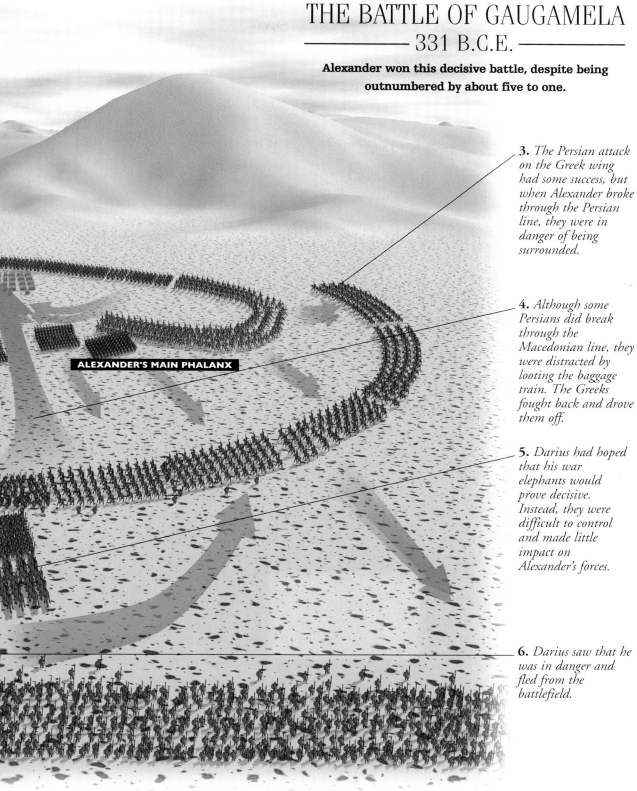

ALEXANDER'S MAIN PHALANX

3. *The Persian attack on the Greek wing had some success, but when Alexander broke through the Persian line, they were in danger of being surrounded.*

4. *Although some Persians did break through the Macedonian line, they were distracted by looting the baggage train. The Greeks fought back and drove them off.*

5. *Darius had hoped that his war elephants would prove decisive. Instead, they were difficult to control and made little impact on Alexander's forces.*

6. *Darius saw that he was in danger and fled from the battlefield.*

Cutting the Gordian Knot

At Gordium, in modern Turkey, there was a large wooden wagon, where the pole of the wagon was fastened to the yoke by a very large and intricate knot. It was said locally that whoever could undo the knot would become the Lord of Asia. Many had tried and failed, but Alexander was determined to succeed and demonstrate that he would soon rule all Asia. Seizing his sword, he slashed through the knot, thus undoing it. Nowadays, we use the phrase "cutting the Gordian Knot" to mean solving a difficult problem.

Alexander is pictured cutting the Gordian Knot in this painting by Jean-Simon Berthélemy (1743–1811).

Alexander now put into operation a dangerous plan. He knew that Darius intended to outflank him and that, to do this, the Persians would reinforce the troops on their wings. These reinforcements could only come from the Persian center. Alexander therefore had to wait until enough troops had moved to the wings so that the Persian center became weak. Then he would attack. However, there was a considerable danger that if he mistimed his attack he would be defeated. If he attacked too early, the Persian center would still be strong, but if he left his attack too late, his own flanks might have been defeated by the Persians, leaving the rest of his army vulnerable. In fact, Alexander's plan succeeded, partly due to the ill discipline of the Persian cavalry. They were too eager to join in the battles on the wings and did not stay to defend the center. With the center weakened, Alexander was able to move forward and defeat Darius. Tens of thousands of the Persians were killed, but only about 1,000 of Alexander's troops died.

Alexander had hoped to capture Darius, but again Darius fled from the battlefield. Alexander now began to consolidate his gains and his grip over the southern parts of the Persian Empire. The southern regions were particularly important because they contained many powerful, wealthy cities as well as the main political centers of the empire. When Alexander had these cities under his control, he would truly be in command of the Persian Empire. Babylon surrendered without resistance. However, Persepolis, the capital of the Persian Empire, was fiercely defended. The capture of Persepolis was a huge psychological gain and also provided Alexander with access to the great store of treasure kept there. Shortly after the city was taken, the palace of Persepolis was burned to the ground. It is not known whether this was done deliberately, in revenge for the damage that the Persians did in Greece during the Persian Wars, or whether it was set on fire by drunken troops.

The Conqueror of the World

In 330 B.C.E., Alexander told the Greek allied soldiers with him that they were now free to return home if they wished. However, many chose to continue to serve with him as paid mercenaries. They were eager to have the opportunity of becoming rich from the loot of the Persian Empire. Alexander now turned his attention toward Afghanistan and India. This was partly because Darius had taken refuge at Ecbatana (modern Hamadan in Iran), the only Persian political center that Alexander had not yet captured. At Alexander's approach, Darius fled and headed toward the Caspian Sea in the region of Bactria (*BAK-tree-uh*). There he was murdered by Bessus, the satrap of Bactria. Bessus now called himself the king of Persia, and Alexander faced a new threat. He dealt with it by cutting off any possible support from the south and pursuing Bessus. In order to isolate Bessus, Alexander crossed a high mountain range that lay in his way. One pass was over 11,000 feet (3,350 meters) high, and to take an army across it showed considerable qualities of leadership and organization. Bessus was forced to retreat further and Alexander eventually caught up with him north of the Oxus River (the modern Amu Darya). Finally, Bessus was betrayed by two local noblemen and handed over to Alexander, who executed him.

For the next two years, from 329 to 327 B.C.E., Alexander was involved in conquering the regions of Bactria and Sogdiana (*SOG-dee-aah-nuh*) in modern Afghanistan and Uzbekistan. There, Alexander faced difficult terrain and a harsh climate. The regions were a mixture of mountain, desert, and steppe. Moreover, Alexander now encountered hit-and-run guerrilla warfare, rather than set-piece battle situations. This sort of war was much harder to fight, and Alexander could no longer claim to be a liberator. Instead, local tribes could say that they were fighting for freedom against an invading conqueror.

Visiting the Oracle at Ammon

The oracle of Ammon was situated in the middle of the desert at the oasis of Siwa. When Alexander visited the oracle, he was greeted by the priest as "the son of Ammon." This was the title of the king of Egypt, so the priest may only have been recognizing that Alexander was the new king. However, Greeks believed that Ammon was the Egyptian version of Zeus, and Alexander's mother, Olympias, had often hinted that he was the son of Zeus. Alexander himself had always believed that Philip could not have been his true father, for how could a mortal man have produced so outstanding a son? Now it seemed that the most important oracle in Egypt had confirmed his special status.

Alexander the God

As Alexander marched through the East, some Greeks thought that he was becoming too dictatorial. In 330 B.C.E., he had one of his loyal generals murdered because the general's son had plotted against him. In 328 B.C.E., Alexander murdered his friend Cleitus (*KLIE-tuss*) in a drunken rage. Cleitus had saved Alexander's life at the Granicus River and many Greeks were shocked at Alexander's behavior. However, what especially angered the Greeks was Alexander's adoption of certain Persian customs, some of which they found deeply offensive. In particular, Alexander ordered everyone who came into his presence to prostrate themselves (or bow down to the floor). This was normal Persian practice when meeting a more important man, but it was greatly resented by the Greeks, who believed that only slaves prostrated themselves before their masters. Free men bowed down only to a god. Therefore, in Greek eyes, either Alexander was treating them as slaves or believed that he was a god. Either possibility appalled the Greeks. Alexander appeared to confirm that he thought he was a god when, in 324 B.C.E., he demanded that the Greek states recognize his divine nature. He also demanded that his great friend Hephaestion (*Heff-EYE-stee-on*), who was now dead, be recognized as a god.

India

After Alexander gained control of Bactria and Sogdiana, he looked toward India. Alexander did not realize how large India was. Indeed, what the ancient Greeks called "India" included both modern India and much of modern Pakistan. Alexander knew of the Punjab, which had once been part of the Persian Empire, and he thought that this was the full extent of Indian territory. He believed that when he had conquered the Punjab, he would reach the Indian Ocean. Alexander wished to see the Indian Ocean, and he also wanted to rule a vast empire. Moving east of the Indus River, Alexander fought and defeated King Porus at the Battle of Hydaspes (*Hi-DASP-eez*, the modern Jhelum River), in 326 B.C.E. It seemed there was nothing to stop Alexander's continued movement east, but when the army reached the Hyphasis (*Hi-FASS-iss*) River, near modern Amritsar, his troops mutinied and refused to go any further. They had faced war elephants, constant fighting, extremely difficult terrain, and monsoon rains. They had fought for eight years and covered 2,000 miles (3,200 kilometers), but still Alexander wished to move on. There seemed to be no end to Alexander's ambition, but the soldiers had had enough and wanted to go home. Alexander was forced to turn back.

365 B.C.E.			350 B.C.E.
Classical Period			
371 Battle of Leuctra Spartans defeated by Thebans	356 Birth of Alexander	359 Philip II becomes king of Macedon	

Alexander now marched down the Indus River to the Arabian Sea. Near modern Karachi, Alexander split his forces. Some returned by an overland route and some went back to Persia by sea. However, Alexander chose to return by a difficult coastal route through a region called Gedrosia (modern southern Iran). This march was a disaster. Far from exploring new routes and finding further supplies of food, the guides lost their way in appalling terrain. Alexander lost touch with his fleet and three-quarters of the men with him died in the harsh desert conditions. Eventually, the army caught up with the fleet and was able to march to the head of the Persian Gulf, where they held a great feast to celebrate.

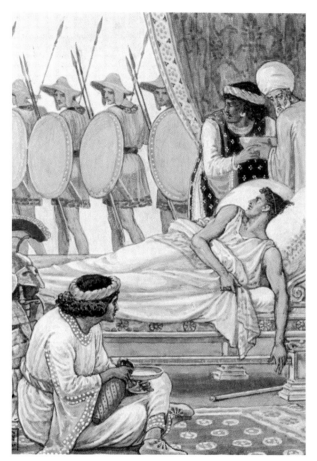

Alexander was only thirty-two years old when he died. His troops were shocked to learn that he was ill and many came to see him in his last hours.

The Death of Alexander

Alexander now intended to explore the coast of Arabia. However, he fell ill in Babylon. After several days' illness, he died at the age of thirty-two. Some people believed that he had been poisoned; others thought that he had died of a fever, made worse by his heavy drinking and the fact that his body was worn out by constant campaigning.

Alexander was a brilliant tactician and a courageous, inspiring leader who won the loyalty of his men. He shared their sufferings and was always at the center of any battle, fighting alongside his troops. However, he was not a good administrator or statesman, nor did he build a lasting empire.

335 B.C.E.		320 B.C.E.	
		Hellenistic Period	
338 Battle of Chaeronea	**331 Battle of Gaugamela**		
335 Alexander destroys Thebes	**329–8 Alexander conquers Bactria and Sogdiana**		
334 Alexander invades Persia **Battle of Granicus River**	**327 Alexander invades India** **326 Battle of Hydaspes**		
336 Alexander becomes king **333 Battle of Issus**	**323 Alexander dies**		

Chapter Five

The Coming of Rome

Although Alexander had been a great general who had conquered most of the known world, his empire did not survive his death. He had not named a successor, stating instead that power should go to the strongest man. This led to over thirty years of fighting between various generals until the empire was divided into three regions. These were Egypt, Asia, and Greece. Egypt was governed by the Ptolemy (*TOLL-uh-mee*) dynasty. Ptolemy I had been one of Alexander's generals and he and his successors ruled Egypt carefully. The vast Asian regions of Alexander's empire were ruled by the Seleucids (*Se-LOO-kids*). The Seleucids were the descendants of another of Alexander's generals, called Seleucus (*Se-LOO-kuss*), and had to fight hard to ensure that they retained control of the region. However, the greatest amount of fighting after Alexander's death was in Greece, where Greek states revolted against Macedonian rule and various generals tried to seize control. The situation was not helped by waves of Celtic tribes invading from the Danube region. Eventually, a strong ruler called Antigonus (*An-TIG-oh-nuss*) gained control of Macedon and, by 272 B.C.E., he had established secure rule and the Antigonid dynasty.

Rome Conquers Greece

In 215 B.C.E., Philip V, king of Macedon, had supported Rome's great enemy, Hannibal of Carthage. Although Rome declared war on Philip, her first concern was to fight Hannibal and, in 205 B.C.E., Rome made peace with Philip. However, Rome was soon to

The kings of Pergamum were very wealthy and spent much money constructing beautiful buildings, such as this temple. Pergamum played a key role in the Roman conquest of Greece.

The Battle of Pydna, 168 B.C.E.
The Phalanx versus the Legion

The Battle of Pydna saw a phalanx of Greek soldiers attempt to defeat Roman legionaries. The Greeks were armed with the long Macedonian spear, or sarissa. Each Roman had a javelin and a short sword known as a gladius (*GLAD-ee-uss*). The main Greek tactic was to deliver a knock-out blow by slamming into the enemy lines and then breaking through. Phalanx attacks of this kind had proved to be decisive in many battles, but there were limitations to how effective they could be.

First, the phalanx was not very maneuverable and was vulnerable to attack on its flanks. If enemy soldiers broke into so tight a formation of troops, it was very difficult for them to defend themselves. These soldiers were so closely packed together that they lacked any room to maneuver. Moreover, it required both hands to hold the heavy sarissa. Thus, the phalanx was normally protected by lighter forces on its flanks. Secondly, the phalanx was only suitable for use on level ground. If it had to charge over rough terrain it risked losing formation. Once its tight formation had been lost, it was easy for enemy soldiers to pick off small groups of men.

At the Battle of Pydna, the Greek troops outnumbered the Romans (44,000 Greeks as opposed to 38,000 Romans). When the battle began, the Roman commander, Paulus, launched an attack on King Perseus' left flank, where there were some weaker forces. The Greek left flank was defeated by effective use of the thirty-four Roman war elephants, but despite this success, the Romans were unable to penetrate the main phalanx. The phalanx then moved forward against the Romans, but the ground was uneven and the attack slowed and finally ground to a halt.

Paulus now ordered his legionaries to attack in small groups. These small groups were much more maneuverable than the massed body of the Greek phalanx and were able to avoid the long sarissas of the Greeks. The Romans were now able to break into the phalanx and attack the Greek soldiers. It was extremely difficult for the Greeks to defend themselves and they began to drop their sarissas in a vain attempt to use their daggers or swords to ward off the enemy. However, while the Roman legionaries were trained for this sort of close combat, the Greeks were not. The phalanx soon broke up into small

The Battle of Pydna demonstrated the superiority of the Roman legion over the Greek phalanx.

sections which were cut to pieces by the Romans. About 25,000 Greeks were said to have been slaughtered or captured (the number may be exaggerated), whereas only 100 Romans died. King Perseus was captured and brought before Paulus. He was later led in triumph through the streets of Rome and died in captivity. The Greek phalanx, once an undefeatable military force, had proved to be unwieldy and inflexible compared to the Roman army.

The Ptolemy Dynasty

The Ptolemies called themselves pharaohs, because they ruled Egypt. However, the Ptolemies were descended from Macedonian nobles and considered themselves to be Greek, not Egyptian. Only the last Ptolemy, Cleopatra VII, spoke Egyptian as well as Greek. Cleopatra was the lover of the Roman general Julius Caesar. After his death she married another important Roman general, Mark Antony. When he was defeated and killed in a Roman civil war, Cleopatra committed suicide.

The Ptolemies were strong supporters of literature and culture. This marble bust is of Ptolemy III, who ruled Egypt from 246–221 B.C.E.

be involved again. Attalus (*AT-uh-luss*), the king of the small state of Pergamum (*PER-guh-mum*), feared the growing power of Philip. He could not ask for help from the Seleucids, who were the local important power, because he knew that they wished to seize his kingdom. The only powerful nation that might help him was Rome. He asked the Romans for help and, in 200 B.C.E., they declared war on Macedon. In 197 B.C.E., Philip was defeated at the Battle of Cynoscephalae (*Kie-no-SKEF-uh-lie*), and was forced to acknowledge Roman authority. When his son, Perseus, became increasingly popular with the Greek states, who did not like Roman rule, Rome again invaded Macedon. Perseus was defeated at the Battle of Pydna (*PID-nuh*) in 168 B.C.E. and the Romans removed the Macedonian kings from power. When the Greeks revolted against Rome in 147 B.C.E., the Romans acted swiftly and defeated the Greek army. Corinth was destroyed by the Romans in 146 B.C.E. and Greece became part of the expanding Roman Empire.

This silver coin dates to the reign of Attalus I of Pergamum (241–197 B.C.E.).

Other parts of Alexander's empire also came into Roman hands. The Seleucid kingdom had gradually weakened and after a defeat in 190 B.C.E., much of the Seleucid territory fell into the hands of the Roman allies of Rhodes and Pergamum. Eventually, Pergamum was left to the people of Rome in Attalus III's will when he died in 133 B.C.E. The Seleucid kingdom was soon reduced to the region of Syria and, in 64 B.C.E., the Roman general, Pompey, seized Syria for Rome. Shortly afterward, in 30 B.C.E., Egypt also became a Roman province.

Although the Romans had conquered Greece and the kingdoms of Alexander's successors, the Romans were greatly impressed by Greek culture. The huge influence that the Greeks had on Roman literature, art, and thought led one Roman author to remark that "Greece, although she was captured, herself captured Rome." The Roman love of all things Greek helped to preserve and to spread Greek culture throughout the world.

King Pyrrhus Invades Italy

During the early third century B.C.E., the Greeks and Romans came into direct conflict. The Romans were putting increasing pressure on the Greek colonies in southern Italy and the colonies appealed to mainland Greece for help. King Pyrrhus (*Pirrus*) of Epirus (*Ee-PEE-russ*) came to their aid and brought an army, including war elephants, to Italy. He defeated the Romans three times, in 280, 279, and 275 B.C.E. However, although he had defeated the Romans, the victories had been won at enormous cost. It is said that, after his second victory over the Romans, he looked around the battlefield. Seeing how many of his own men lay dead he remarked, "If I have another such victory I shall be sailing back to Greece on my own." This is the origin of the phrase "a Pyrrhic victory," meaning a victory won at such cost that it is effectively a defeat.

King Pyrrhus of Epirus was a cousin of Alexander the Great and defeated the Romans in battle in Italy.

Glossary of Names

Alcibiades (around 450–404 B.C.E.) Athenian general

Alexander the Great (356–323 B.C.E.) king of Macedon, son of Philip II

Amompharetus Spartan general at the Battle of Plataea, 479 B.C.E.

Antigonus II ruler of Macedon from 277–239 B.C.E.

Apollo god of the sun

Aristotle (384–322 B.C.E.) philosopher and tutor of Alexander the Great

Attalus king of Pergamum from 241–197 B.C.E.

Bessus satrap (governor) of Bactria and claimant to the Persian throne in 330 B.C.E.

Brasidas (around 472–422 B.C.E.) Spartan general in the Peloponnesian War

Bucephalus Alexander the Great's horse

Callimachus Athenian chief general at the Battle of Marathon, 490 B.C.E.

Cambyses king of Persia from 529–522 B.C.E., son of Cyrus the Great

Cleitus (around 380–328 B.C.E.) friend of Alexander the Great

Cleomenes (around 520–489 B.C.E.) Spartan king during the Ionian Revolt

Cleopatra VII (69–30 B.C.E.) pharaoh of Egypt

Croesus king of Lydia from 560–546 B.C.E.

Cyrus the Great king of Persia from 560–529 B.C.E.

Darius I king of Persia from 552–486 B.C.E., cousin of Cambyses

Darius III king of Persia from 336–330 B.C.E.

Demosthenes (around 460–413 B.C.E.) Athenian general in the Peloponnesian War

Demosthenes (384–322 B.C.E.) Athenian orator who opposed Philip II of Macedon

Ephialtes Greek traitor who showed the Persians a secret path at Thermopylae

Eucles Athenian runner who may have announced the victory at Marathon in 490 B.C.E.

Euripides (around 485–406 B.C.E.) Athenian dramatist

Gylippus Spartan advisor to the Syracusans in 414 B.C.E.

Hannibal (around 246–182 B.C.E.) Carthaginian general and enemy of Rome

Hephaestion (around 356–324 B.C.E.) friend of Alexander the Great

Herodotus (484–around 425 B.C.E.) the first historian, author of a history of the Persian Wars

Homer (eighth century B.C.E.) blind poet, author of the *Iliad* and the *Odyssey*

Julius Caesar (100–44 B.C.E.) Roman general

Lamachus (died in 414 B.C.E.) Athenian general in Sicily during the Peloponnesian War

Leonidas king of Sparta from around 489–480 B.C.E.; died at the Battle of Thermopylae

Lysander (died in 395 B.C.E.) Spartan general during the Peloponnesian War

Mardonius Persian commander during the Persian Wars and son-in-law of Darius I

Mark Antony (around 82–30 B.C.E.) Roman general and lover of Cleopatra VII

Miltiades Athenian general at the Battle of Marathon, 490 B.C.E.

Nicias (around 470–413 B.C.E.) Athenian general in Sicily during the Peloponnesian War

Olympias Alexander the Great's mother, divorced from Philip II of Macedon

Pan god of shepherds and forests

Paulus Roman general at the Battle of Pydna, 168 B.C.E.

Pausanius Spartan king and leader at the Battle of Plataea, 479 B.C.E.

Pericles (around 495–429 B.C.E.) Athenian leader during much of the mid-fifth-century B.C.E.

Perseus son of Philip V of Macedon and king from 179–168 B.C.E.

Pheidippides Athenian runner who may have announced the victory at Marathon in 490 B.C.E.

Philip II king of Macedon from 359–336 B.C.E. and father of Alexander the Great

Philip V king of Macedon from 221–179 B.C.E.

Pisistratus ruler of Athens from 546–527 B.C.E.

Pompey (106–48 B.C.E.) Roman general who took control of Syria for Rome

Porus king in eastern Punjab, defeated by Alexander the Great in 326 B.C.E.

Ptolemy Macedonian general and king of Egypt after the death of Alexander the Great

Pyrrhus (319–272 B.C.E.) king of Epirus who fought the Romans in Italy and Sicily

Seleucus Macedonian general who gained control of much of the eastern empire after Alexander's death

Simonides (around 556–468 B.C.E.) Greek poet and author of the epitaph for the dead of Thermopylae

Socrates (469–399 B.C.E.) Athenian philosopher

Themistocles (c. 528–462 B.C.E.) Athenian admiral during the Persian Wars

Thucydides (around 460–400 B.C.E.) Athenian historian of the Peloponnesian War

Xerxes king of Persia from 486–465 B.C.E; defeated by the Greeks in the Persian Wars

Glossary

acropolis the fortified part of a city, built on high ground

arbitration an outsider's opinion in a dispute

attrition the wearing down of an enemy over time

breastplate piece of armor worn to protect the chest

butt-spike a spike on the base of a spear shaft

catapult a machine used to throw rocks or other heavy objects

Companions Alexander the Great's elite Macedonian cavalry

conscript a soldier who has been compulsorily enlisted rather than having volunteered

cuirass stiffened linen armor to protect the chest

cyclops a one-eyed giant

democracy rule by the majority of voters

eclipse one planet or star passing in front of another

flax fiber made from the stalks of a plant

gladius short sword used by a Roman legionary

gorgon a mythical female monster with snakes for hair

greaves leg protectors

Guards Alexander the Great's elite Macedonian infantry

helepolis giant siege engine used in the siege of Rhodes

Helots slaves of Sparta

hoplites heavily armed infantrymen

Immortals Persian troops, known for their courage

imperialist someone who believes in and encourages the expansion of a state's influence and colonization of new territory by its citizens

infantrymen soldiers equipped and trained to fight on foot

mercenary a professional soldier who fought for whoever paid him, rather than someone or something in which he believed

oligarchy rule by a few select people

oracle a shrine where the future may be foretold

paean a war-song

peltasts lightly armed Macedonican troops

pentecontor ship with fifty oars

Perioikoi Spartan inhabitants who were neither full citizens nor slaves

phalanx a special formation of infantry in close ranks

pharaoh Egyptian ruler

plague a disease that spreads rapidly and kills many people

professional someone who is paid for what they do, such as a poet who writes for money, not just for pleasure

prostrate bow down to the floor

prow the bow, or front of a ship

sacrilege disrespect for something considered sacred

sarissa a type of Macedonian spear

satrap a local or provincial governor in the ancient Persian Empire

scythe a curved blade

siege surrounding of a city or area by enemy troops

soothsayer a prophet; one who can foretell events

Spartiates Spartan citizens

steppe flat, unforested grassland

temple a building used for prayer and worship

trireme warship with 170 rowers

Learn More About

Books

Anglim, Simon, and Phyllis Jestice, Rob Rice, Scott Rusch, John Serrati. *Fighting Techniques of the Ancient World*. New York: St. Martin's Press, 2002.

Biesty, Stephen. *Greece in Spectacular Cross-Section*. Oxford: Oxford University Press, 2006.

Chrisp, Peter. *Alexander the Great—Legend of a Warrior King*. New York: Dorling Kindersley, 2003.

Connolly, Peter. *Greece and Rome at War*. Mechanicsburg, PA: Stackpole Books, 1998.

de Souza, Philip. *The Peloponnesian War 431–404 B.C.* New York: Routledge, 2003.

Heckel, Waldermar. *The Wars of Alexander the Great, 336–323 B.C.* New York: Routledge, 2003.

Sekunda, Nicholas. *Greek Hoplite, 480–323 B.C.* Oxford: Osprey, 2000.

Warry, John. *Alexander the Great*. Oxford: Osprey, 2001.

Warry, John. *Warfare in the Classical World*. Norman, Oklahoma: University of Oklahoma Press, 1995.

Woods, Michael and Mary Woods. *Ancient Warfare: From Clubs to Catapults*. Minneapolis, Minnesota: Runestone Press, 2000.

Web Sites

About.com—Greek Warfare
http://ancienthistory.about.com/od/greekweapons/Greek_Soldiers_Hoplites.htm

Boise State University—The Peloponnesian War
http://history.boisestate.edu/westciv/peloponn/

British Museum—Ancient Greece
www.ancient-greece.co.uk

Eyewitness to History—Alexander
www.eyewitnesstohistory.com/alexander.htm

Eyewitness to History—Battle of Marathon
www.eyewitnesstohistory.com/marathon.htm

HistoryWiz—Ancient Greece
www.historywiz.com/anc-greece.htm

Kidipede—Ancient Greek Warfare
http://www.historyforkids.org/learn/greeks/war/index.htm

King Leonidas and the 300 Spartans of Thermoplyae
http://300spartanwarriors.com

Olympia Museum
www.culture.gr/2/21/211/21107m/e211gm04.html

World News Network—Ancient Greece
www.ancientgreece.com

Glossary of Ancient Greek Military Terms
http://members.tripod.com/~S_van_Dorst/Ancient_Warfare/Greece/greek_glossary.html

Index